POLICY ANALYSES IN INTERNATIONAL ECONOMICS 15

TRADE POLICY FOR TROUBLED INDUSTRIES

Gary Clyde Hufbauer
and
Howard F. Rosen

INSTITUTE FOR INTERNATIONAL ECONOMICS
WASHINGTON, DC
MARCH 1986

Gary Clyde Hufbauer was a Senior Fellow at the Institute until August 1985 when he became Marcus Wallenberg Professor of International Financial Diplomacy at Georgetown University. Hufbauer was formerly Deputy Assistant Secretary for International Trade and Investment Policy of the US Treasury; Director of the International Tax Staff at the Treasury; and Professor of Economics at the University of New Mexico.

Howard F. Rosen is a Research Associate and Assistant to the Director at the Institute. He was formerly an international economist at the US Department of Labor.

The authors would like to acknowledge all the participants in this multiyear project. Our work was greatly influenced by discussions of our three working groups on labor adjustment, industry adjustment, and trade policy. An earlier draft of this manuscript had the benefit of comments from C. Michael Aho, Isabel Sawhill, Robert J. Flanagan, and Malcolm Lovell. We are grateful for the intellectual input and encouragement we received from Thomas O. Bayard throughout this project. Numerous drafts were typed by Debbie McGuire and Donna Edmonds, and Kimberly Ann Elliott's continued research assistance and attention to detail were indispensable.

G.C.H.   H.F.R.

INSTITUTE FOR INTERNATIONAL ECONOMICS

C. Fred Bergsten, *Director*
Kathleen A. Lynch, *Director of Publications*

The Institute for International Economics was created, and is principally funded, by the German Marshall Fund of the United States.

Library of Congress Cataloging-in-Publication Data
Hufbauer, Gary Clyde.
Trade policy for troubled industries
(Policy analyses in international economics; 15)

Bibliography: p. 95
1. United States—Commercial policy. 2. Commercial policy—Case studies. 3. Free trade and protection—Protection. I. Rosen, Howard F. II. Title.
HF1455.H787   1986   382'.3'0973   85–18105
ISBN 0-88132-020-X

TRADE POLICY FOR TROUBLED INDUSTRIES

Contents

Preface

In a major research project over the past two years, the Institute has studied the postwar adjustment to trade competition of troubled industries in the United States and in five other countries. Common themes have been sought that may warn of the onset of competitive problems, permitting both industries and public policy to address them more rapidly. Lessons have been drawn from the adjustment efforts of the past to help devise effective remedies for the future. This study presents the major analytical conclusions and policy recommendations resulting from the entire study.

The adjustment project, directed by Gary Clyde Hufbauer and Howard F. Rosen, will produce three publications. In addition to this one, we are concurrently releasing *Trade Protection in the United States: 31 Case Studies,* which provides detailed analyses of cases in which trade volumes exceed $100 million and the United States has applied "special" trade protection—exceptional restraints on imports through high tariffs, quotas, or other unusual limitations. *Domestic Adjustment and International Trade,* scheduled for release later in 1986, will contain the papers commissioned on specific aspects of the problem (including adjustment experiences abroad). (Some of the central conclusions of this project were cited in *Trading for Growth: The Next Round of Trade Negotiations,* by Dr. Hufbauer and Jeffrey J. Schott, released by the Institute in September 1985.)

The Ford Foundation provided substantial support for the entire adjustment project, and I would like to convey a special word of thanks for its help. In particular, all of the researchers engaged in this effort at the Institute wish to express their gratitude to Thomas O. Bayard, a Foundation Program Officer, for his important intellectual inputs to the project—on a topic to which he has made a number of pioneering contributions in the past.

The Institute for International Economics is a private nonprofit research institution for the study and discussion of international economic policy. Its purpose is to analyze important issues in that area and to develop and communicate practical new approaches for dealing with them. The Institute is completely nonpartisan.

The Institute was created in November 1981 through a generous commitment of funds from the German Marshall Fund of the United States. Support is being received from other private foundations and corporations, and the Institute is now broadening and diversifying its financial base. As noted, the Ford Foundation provided substantial support for this study.

The Board of Directors bears overall responsibility for the Institute and gives general guidance and approval to its research program—including identification of topics that are likely to become important to international economic policymakers over the medium run (generally, one to three years) and which thus should be addressed by the Institute. The Director, working closely with the staff and outside Advisory Committee, is responsible for the development of particular projects and makes the final decision to publish an individual study.

The Institute hopes that its studies and other activities will contribute to building a stronger foundation for international economic policy around the world. Comments as to how it can best do so are invited from readers of these publications.

C. FRED BERGSTEN
Director
March 1986

1 Introduction

With bipartisan regularity, American presidents since Franklin D. Roosevelt have proclaimed the virtues of free trade. They have inaugurated bold international programs to reduce tariff and nontariff barriers. But almost in the same breath, most presidents have advocated or accepted special measures to protect problem industries. Together, these two strands of policy have produced a contradictory profile. On one hand, the United States has dramatically liberalized its tariff barriers since the Smoot–Hawley Tariff of 1930.[1] On the other, the United States has imposed numerous regimes of "special protection" to insulate manufacturing and agriculture from foreign competition.

In recent years, and in some past periods, dollar overvaluation and high unemployment have dramatically heightened the cry for special protection; but the underlying quest transcends year-to-year fluctuations in the exchange rate and the business cycle. Early in the twentieth century, important instances of special protection included book manufacturing, the maritime industry, and sugar. In the post–World War II period, Presidents Dwight D. Eisenhower and John F. Kennedy launched America on a new trajectory of special protection, first with "voluntary" restraints on Japanese exports of cotton textiles that ripened into the Short-Term and Long-Term Cotton Textile Arrangements, and then with voluntary and mandatory controls on oil imports. President Lyndon B. Johnson ushered in the legal apparatus for restricting meat and steel imports. In the wake of oil scarcity, President Richard Nixon allowed oil import controls to lapse, but he also continued to restrain steel imports and tightened textile restrictions with the first Multi-Fiber Arrangement. President Gerald R. Ford contributed specialty steel to the agenda of special protection, but little else, mainly because his short tenure in office coincided with the inauguration of the Tokyo Round of Multilateral Trade

---

1. The ratio of duties collected to dutiable imports dropped from 53.5 percent in 1933 to 5.2 percent in 1982 (US Trade Representative 1984, p. 187).

1

Negotiations. As part of the price for implementing the Tokyo Round agreements, however, President Jimmy Carter restricted imports of steel, tightened restraints on textiles and apparel, and introduced restrictions on footwear and TVs. During his first term, President Ronald Reagan answered the prayers of the sugar, textile and apparel, automobile, and steel industries.

In short, the US response to the trade and structural problems of important industries has often been special protection. The purpose of special protection is to slow the pace of adjustment to changing realities in the international marketplace, especially for industries that are already experiencing the aging pains of maturity.[2]

The United States is not the only country to have experienced competition in mature industries from foreign goods. Most industrial countries, in Europe, Japan, and elsewhere, have encountered similar difficulties. Various nations have tried different admixtures of consolidation, subsidies, and protection to address the problems of their mature industries.[3]

Broadly speaking, how have these programs worked? Any assessment critically depends on the definition of "successful adjustment." In our view, a successful adjustment program is a temporary program that, within 5 or 10 years, ensures that the industry can once again meet international competition without further government intervention and that labor has been reemployed elsewhere in the economy.

The experience of industrial countries with troubled industries suggests three clear conclusions, judged against these "success" criteria. First, protection against trade pressure often lasts far longer than necessary for adjustment of the *existing* labor force. Second, there are very few instances where temporary protection has fostered a "phoenix" industry that could

---

2. A large literature has developed that seeks to explain the "political market" for protection. Among the variables emphasized are numbers of employees, value added per employee, degree of concentration, extent of financial adversity, and import share. For example: Magee (1980); Messerlin (1981); Anderson and Baldwin (1981); Baldwin (1984a and 1984b); Cline (1984a); Cassing, McKeown, and Ochs (1984); and Pugel and Walter (1983). The premise of this study is that the "political market" can be reshaped by meaningful alternatives to protection. I. M. Destler and John Odell are currently working on an Institute project using these same variables to determine the political market *against* protection.

3. This survey is based on papers that will appear in Hufbauer and Rosen (1986b). These papers examine industry adjustment experience in Australia, Germany, Japan, the United Kingdom, and the United States, and labor adjustment experience in Germany, Japan, Sweden, and the United States.

regain its erstwhile share of the domestic market or maintain its former level of employment without indefinite government protection. Third, in some instances, protection has furthered consolidation and modernization that led to a smaller but stronger core of firms that appear able to survive without continued protection. These are the achievable "success stories" in the annals of public policy for troubled industries.

Experience with integrated carbon steel production, an industry that has come to symbolize industrial decline, illustrates the converse of successful adjustment. In three major countries—the United States, the United Kingdom, and Germany—trade protection and other assistance measures have been justified by images of new investment that would avert steel shortages and lead to the revitalization of old mills. The economic reality has been an extensive and pervasive decline of demand, made worse by competition from low-cost suppliers both abroad (primarily developing countries) and at home (mini-mills). Governments have used different methods to deal with this competition, ranging from huge subsidies for a state producer (British Steel Corporation), to sporadic trade protection (the United States), to permanent trade protection coupled with large subsidies (the Federal Republic of Germany). None of these strategies has succeeded in enabling firms to compete with Korean or Japanese steel.

This monograph examines various means of dealing with troubled industries, some more successful than others. In chapter 2, we examine US experience with trade protection as a means of dealing with the problems of trade-impacted industries. The United States has invented multiple roads to "special protection" for troubled industries, ranging from exceptionally high tariffs, to presidential use of constitutional prerogatives, to congressional quotas, to relief administered by the United States International Trade Commission (USITC). Surveying 31 significant cases of special protection, we examine various characteristics—for example, the use of quantitative restraints, the extent of trade coverage, the duration of protection, and the cost of protection.

In chapter 3, we look at the labor side of adjustment. Most industrial countries experienced slow growth and rising unemployment following the Organization of Petroleum Exporting Countries (OPEC) oil shock of 1973. This climate made labor adjustment generally difficult. Among industrial countries, the United States has the least developed system of special measures for displaced workers. Beyond a general program of unemployment insurance, US measures are small both in scope and funding. Trade Adjustment

Assistance (TAA) was never very large and has now practically disappeared from the budgetary landscape.

In chapter 4, we look at other alternatives (besides TAA) to long-term protection tried in the United States, namely temporary "escape clause" assistance, antitrust policy, and tax policy. Although flawed in their implementation, these alternatives are far more constructive than long-term protection; consequently, they furnish useful building blocks for a new approach.

Finally, in chapter 5, we outline a new alternative to special protection that could be implemented by the United States. The new approach emphasizes protection that is degressive over time, with revenues derived from trade protection dedicated to the adjustment needs of the industry. The new approach is placed in an international context of interlocking obligations undertaken by the major trading powers.

2 Special Protection in the United States

Since World War II, the US government has relied heavily on "special protection" for individual industries facing severe import competition. By "special protection," we mean exceptional restraints on imports, implemented through high tariffs, quotas, or other limitations that go well beyond normal tariff or border restrictions. With increasing use, special protection has gained wider intellectual acceptance in trade policy circles. Yet the costs of this policy approach, when weighed against alternative ways of dealing with troubled industries, are very high. In 1984, ongoing cases of special protection cost US consumers approximately $56 billion. In that year, the efficiency loss to the entire economy was about $8 billion.

Table 2.1 summarizes 31 significant cases of US special protection. We have arbitrarily defined "significant" cases as those that affect trade in excess of $100 million. Based on these cases, certain general themes can be drawn about the roads to special protection and the characteristics of special protection in the United States.

Routes to Special Protection

The US Constitution explicitly entrusts the regulation of foreign commerce to the Congress and implicitly entrusts the conduct of foreign affairs to the President (Tribe 1978, pp. 165–67). Thus, the constitutional schema assigns roles to both the President and Congress in formulating international trade policy. Familiar scenes characterize the way these two branches of government play their roles when they confront industries seeking special protection.

In the first scene, the President customarily resists protectionist solutions. He points to the costs of protection, America's international commitments, and the virtues of self-help. If the industry is politically ineffective, or recovers its economic health, that usually ends the drama. However, if the

5

industry is politically strong yet continues to reel from competition at home and cheaper goods from abroad, congressional pressure often builds for relief.

In the second scene, key senators and congressmen urge the industry's case. To emphasize their interest, the lawmakers may attach riders to legislation needed by the administration.

In the third scene, the President sees his political goals endangered, and grudgingly comes to accept the case for trade restraint. But the President tries to build maximum flexibility into the regime so that restrictions may be liberalized as economic and political winds change.

The fourth and final scene is an apologia, in which the President defends his program as less protective than the solutions threatened by Congress.

So much for common scenes. The cases in table 2.1 illustrate five distinct legal paths to special protection. These are summarized in the next few sections.

EXCEPTIONALLY HIGH TARIFFS

In the 1920s and 1930s, high tariffs were the main answer to troublesome competition from foreign quarters. The high tariffs remaining today are largely a legacy from the Fordney–McCumber Tariff Act of 1922 and the Smoot–Hawley Tariff Act of 1930, retained by industries with sufficient political strength to guard their ancestral ramparts against the erosion of seven rounds of trade liberalization under the auspices of the General Agreement on Tariffs and Trade (GATT). Prior to each tariff-cutting round, certain industries have managed to persuade Congress that they cannot survive without their accustomed tariffs. This prejudgment may be given legal sanction by specific exclusion from the President's tariff-cutting authority;[1] or it may be conveyed by a special investigation that identifies "import-sensitive" industries;[2] or it may be urged informally but persuasively to the President by key senators and congressmen.

---

1. For example, section 127 of the Trade Act of 1974 exempted goods subject to escape clause relief, and certain other goods, from tariff cuts. A similar exemption was first used in section 225 of the Trade Expansion Act of 1962 (Metzger 1964, p. 41).

2. The Trade Agreements Extension Act of 1951 required the US Tariff Commission (established in 1916 and transformed in 1975 into the US International Trade Commission) to designate "peril points" beyond which tariffs could not be safely cut. The Trade Expansion Act of 1962 eliminated the "peril point" terminology but required the Tariff Commission to designate "import-sensitive" industries. In both cases, while the designation was not binding on the President, it carried weight (Metzger 1971a, pp. 320–21).

TABLE 2.1 **Characteristics of special protection**

Case	Route and termination[a] (symbols)	Relief period[b] (dates)	Import value (million dollars)	Tariff or equivalent (percentage)	Induced increase in domestic price (percentage)	Induced decrease in imports (million dollars)	Induced increase in employment[c]
Manufacturing							
M-1 Book Manufacturing	(E), (1)	1891–present	481 (1984)	40.0	12.0	421	5,000
M-2 Benzenoid Chemicals	(A), (1)	1922–86	2,698 (1984)	15.0	4.5	750	300
M-3 Glassware	(A), (1)	1922–present	312 (1983)	19.0	12.0	118	1,000
M-4 Rubber Footwear	(A), (1)	1930–present	331 (1983)	42.0	21.0	125	7,800
M-5 Ceramic Articles	(A, B), (1)	1930–present	498 (1984)	14.0	7.0	126	2,000
M-6 Ceramic Tiles	(A), (1)	1930–present	249 (1984)	21.6	17.3	66	850
M-7 Orange Juice	(A), (1)	1930–present	304 (1983)	44.0	35.0	363	2,200
M-8 Canned Tuna	(A), (1)	1951–present	137 (1983)	12.5	10.0	52	1,200
M-9 Textiles and Apparel: Phase I	(A, D), (1)	1957–73	3,497 (1973)	20.0	16.0	8,600	420,000
M-10 Textiles and Apparel: Phase II	(A, D), (1)	1974–81	9,500 (1981)	27.0	22.0	15,000	540,000
M-11 Textiles and Apparel: Phase III	(A, D), (1)	1982–present	16,498 (1984)	30.0	24.0	27,900	640,000
M-12 Carbon Steel: Phase I	(C), (2)	1969–74	4,830 (1974)	13.3	5.3	1,420	8,100
M-13 Carbon Steel: Phase II	(C, D), (1)	1978–82	8,958 (1982)	15.9	6.4	2,146	7,000
M-14 Carbon Steel: Phase III	(B, C, D), (1)	1982–present	10,206 (1984)	30.0	12.0	3,038	9,000
M-15 Ball Bearings	(B), (2)	1974–78	199 (1978)	12.0	2.4	6	500

TABLE 2.1 **Characteristics of special protection** (continued)

Case	Route and termination[a] (symbols)	Relief period[b] (dates)	Import value (million dollars)	Tariff or equivalent (percentage)	Induced increase in domestic price (percentage)	Induced decrease in imports (million dollars)	Induced increase in employment[c]
Manufacturing							
M–16 Specialty Steel	(B), (3) (B), (1)	1976–80 1983–86	404 (1984)	25.0	15.0	77	500
M–17 Nonrubber Footwear	(B), (3)	1977–81	2,480 (1981)	18.5	5.5	248	12,700
M–18 Color Televisions	(B), (3)	1977–82	1,543 (1982)	15.0	6.0	125	1,000
M–19 CB Radios	(B), (3)	1978–81	54 (1981)	21.0	21.0	132	600
M–20 Bolts, Nuts, Large Screws	(B), (3)	1979–82	311 (1982)	15.0	6.0	10	200
M–21 Prepared Mushrooms[d]	(B), (3)	1980–83	110 (1983)	20.0	10.0	16	300
M–22 Automobiles	(C), (1)	1981–present[e]	29,260 (1984)	11.0	4.4	5,800	55,000
M–23 Motorcycles	(B), (1)	1983–1988	124 (1984)	30.0	15.0	163	700
Services							
S–1 Maritime Industries[f]	(E), (1)	1789–present	15,000 (1983)	0.0	60.0	7,000	11,000
Agriculture and Fisheries							
A–1 Sugar	(D), (1)	1934–present	1,258 (1984)	30.0	30.0	1,288	15,300 1,350,000 (acres)
A–2 Dairy Products	(D), (1)	1953–present	588 (1983)	80.0	40.0	2,300	25,000 3,000,000 (cows)
A–3 Peanuts	(D), (1)	1953–present	2 (1983)	28.0	28.0	200	170,000 (acres)

A–4 Meat	(D), (1)	1965–present	1,363 (1983)	14.0	7.0	1,500	11,000 8,000,000 (head)
A–5 Fish	(E), (1)	1977–present	3,627 (1983)	10.0	10.0	280	27,000
Mining							
E–1 Petroleum	(D), (2)	1959–73	7,858 (1973)	96.0	96.0	6,550	43,000
E–2 Lead and Zinc	(B), (2)	1958–65	141 (1964)	9.5	9.5	45	2,200

a. The symbols used to identify the route of initiation of special protection are as follows: A—high tariffs; B—escape clause action; C—executive use of inherent constitutional powers (e.g., voluntary export restraints); D—statutory framework for discretionary protection (e.g., section 22 of the Agricultural Adjustment Act of 1933); E—statutes explicitly limiting imports (e.g., the Magnuson Act restricting foreign fishing in the US Fishery Conservation Zone). The symbols used to identify the means of termination of special protection are as follows: 1—not applicable as protection is either ongoing or has been replaced by another phase or means of relief; 2—protection terminated because of a revival of demand and/or an increase in prices; 3—protection terminated or phased out following industry adjustment through downsizing, product shifts, and/or reinvestment and modernization.

b. Termination dates in currently ongoing cases assume that tariffs are lowered and other types of protection are phased out as scheduled.

c. Unless otherwise specified, figures refer to the number of production jobs.

d. Prepared mushrooms have been treated only as an escape clause case even though the relatively high ad valorem equivalent (13.3 percent in 1984) makes it a borderline high tariff case as well.

e. The automobile case is defined as ongoing and in need of adjustment because of continuing Japanese export restraint.

f. Import values are for the shipping services sector only. There was no increase in import prices since protection was implemented through subsidization and cargo reservation.

The average US tariff on dutiable imports has now dwindled to about 5 percent. By contrast, the tariff-based instances of special protection singled out in table 2.1 involve tariffs of about 15 percent and higher. These self-selected survivors of the Fordney-McCumber and Smoot-Hawley tariffs include Benzenoid Chemicals, Rubber Footwear, Ceramic Articles and Tiles, Glassware, Canned Tuna, Textiles and Apparel (Phases I, II, and III), and Orange Juice.[3] The Textile and Apparel cases and the Ceramic Articles case involve additional forms of protection besides high tariffs. In terms of trade coverage, the big case is Textiles and Apparel: Phase III, involving $16.5 billion of imports in 1984. Benzenoid Chemicals is next at $2.7 billion in 1984. After that, the high tariff cases entail trade coverages in the hundreds of millions of dollars.

ESCAPE CLAUSE RELIEF

Now granted under section 201 of the Trade Act of 1974,[4] the escape clause in theory was meant to provide the major route to special protection. In practice, escape clause relief has become a secondary road. The award of escape clause relief is highly discretionary and relief has been granted far less often than it has been sought. Moreover, the escape clause contains features that are disagreeable to industry: it contemplates the decline of protection from year to year and the corresponding adjustment of the petitioning industry to the realities of international competition.

---

3. The case names used here and later in this chapter are the names used in Hufbauer, Berliner, and Elliott (1986). The high-tariff cases listed in table 2.1 do not give a representative sample of the history of high tariffs as an instrument of special protection, since troubled industries that had their high tariffs cut prior to 1984 are not listed.

4. Section 201 of the Trade Act of 1974 was preceded by several earlier versions of an escape clause: an industry consultation provision in the Reciprocal Trade Agreements Act of 1934; a formal "escape clause" in the 1942 bilateral trade agreement with Mexico; Executive Order 9832 of 1945 in which President Harry S Truman required that an escape clause be included in all future trade agreements; a legislative escape clause in section 7 of the Trade Agreements Extension Act of 1951; and a revised escape clause in section 301 of the Trade Expansion Act of 1962. The 1962 Act required that trade concessions be the major cause of increased imports and that rising imports be a "major factor" in causing or threatening injury; the 1974 Act dropped the linkage to trade concessions and relaxed the causation test to "substantial cause" (US International Trade Commission 1982, pp. 1–4; Metzger 1971a, pp. 319–21; Baldwin 1984a, ch. 3).

An industry seeking escape clause relief must clear two hurdles. First, the industry must persuade the US International Trade Commission (USITC) to find that the industry has been "seriously injured" or "threatened" with serious injury, and that rising imports are the most important cause of the actual injury or the threat of injury. Second, once half or more of the commissioners sitting on the case recommend trade relief, the industry must persuade the President that trade relief serves the national interest more than adjustment assistance or, indeed, no relief at all.

From 1975 to 1984, some 53 import-relief petitions were brought to the USITC under sections 201 and 203 (section 203 enables an extension of prior relief) (Baldwin 1984b, p. 19). A majority of the Commission recommended trade relief in 28 instances and the Commission was evenly split on 3 cases. Of these 31 cases (28 plus 3), the President granted trade relief in only 13 cases. Some of these 13 cases involved too little trade coverage to qualify as significant instances of special protection.[5] Significant instances of escape clause relief and end-year trade coverage include Ball Bearings ($199 million in 1978); Specialty Steel ($404 million in 1984); Nonrubber Footwear ($2,480 million in 1981); Color Televisions ($1,543 million in 1982); Mushrooms ($110 million in 1983); Motorcycles ($124 million in 1984); CB Radios ($54 million in 1981);[6] Bolts, Nuts, and Large Screws ($311 million in 1982); and Ceramic Articles ($498 million in 1984).

Adjustment under the escape clause is often more successful than adjustment under other routes. Because this experience holds important lessons, escape clause cases are discussed in greater detail in chapter 4.

PRESIDENTIAL USE OF INHERENT CONSTITUTIONAL POWERS

The President may use his inherent responsibility for the conduct of foreign policy to persuade foreign governments to limit their exports to the United States using administrative means. This low-visibility, high-flexibility form

---

5. Recent escape clause relief cases that resulted in trade restrictions but did not involve significant amounts of trade include: Ferrochromium (TA–201–35); Clothespins (TA–201–36); and Non-Electric Cookware (TA–201–39).

6. CB radio imports totaled $194 million in 1978, the first year of restraints. The large decline in subsequent years was due principally to declining demand for a "fad" item, rather than to trade restraints.

of protection has become a favored means of helping large troubled industries. The President can claim credit both for defending the principles of free trade (against more protective congressional or USITC solutions) and for defending the industry (against the "dangers" of unregulated commerce); moreover, this form of protection could enable the President to more easily conceal the cost of protection from the public. In addition, the President can compensate foreign exporters by assigning them the economic rents created by quantitative restraints and he can relax or remove the restraints rather easily once political attitudes or economic fortunes change.

An early example of the use of inherent constitutional powers was President Lyndon B. Johnson's steel restraints (Carbon Steel: Phase I). The latest example was President Ronald Reagan's use of voluntary restraint agreements (VRAs) to limit steel shipments by the European Community, Brazil, Korea, Spain, Japan, and other suppliers (Carbon Steel: Phase III). Another example was President Reagan's auto restraints.

As these examples indicate, the trade-coverage figures can be huge. It is no accident that VRAs are often used when the trade stakes are large. Damage control of diplomatic consequences is a major reason that presidents use their inherent constitutional powers to deal with such cases.

STATUTORY FRAMEWORKS FOR DISCRETIONARY PROTECTION

Statutory frameworks often seem to give the President considerable latitude in deciding how to answer the trade problems of affected industries. In practice, that latitude may be narrowed by congressional surveillance. Examples are section 204 of the Agricultural Act of 1956, used as the statutory vehicle for restraining textile and apparel imports, and section 22 of the Agricultural Adjustment Act of 1933 (1935 amendment), currently used to limit dairy, peanut, cotton, and sugar imports.[7] In deploying both these statutes, presidents pay close attention to congressional sentiment.

Another statute, section 232 of the Trade Expansion Act of 1962, permits trade restrictions for national security purposes. Section 232 was used to restrain petroleum imports between 1962 and 1973. More recently, the bolts, nuts, and large screws industry, and the machine tool industry have tried— so far without success—to harness section 232 to their protective desires.

---

7. Since its enactment in 1935, section 22 has been used, from time to time, to restrict imports of cotton, wheat, almonds, dairy, peanuts, flaxseed, filberts, oats, rye, barley, tungnuts, and sugar (Congressional Research Service 1984, p. 9).

Unusual quantitative relief in countervailing duty and antidumping duty cases is the latest variety of extraordinary restraint applied within a statutory framework. This approach was inaugurated in 1978 by the trigger price mechanism (Carbon Steel: Phase II). The same approach was followed in the settlement of subsidy complaints against Chinese textiles in 1983 (Textiles and Apparel: Phase III). Indeed, in recent years, most successful import quota campaigns have been preceded by dumping or subsidy cases producing eye-catching margins.[8] In 1984 and 1985, this happened with steel from virtually all countries except Japan and Korea; and in 1986, it promises to happen with Japanese semiconductors. Aggressive pursuit of the antidumping and countervailing duty remedies drives foreign producers to the quota bargaining table. Moreover, once foreign producers are subject to a quota regime, they often wish to expand the regime to cover third-country competitors.

STATUTORY QUOTAS

These statutes represent the most decisive exercise of congressional power. They often set a rigid limit on imports, expressed as a percentage of consumption or as a residual between domestic consumption and domestic production, or they altogether bar foreign suppliers from the US market. Examples include the manufacturing clause of the copyright law, the Jones Act, the Meat Act, and the Magnuson Fisheries Act. Each of these laws strictly limits foreign entry, allowing presidential discretion only as to details of implementation. It is worth noting, however, that statutory quotas are threatened far more frequently than they are enacted. The most recent setback to this form of trade restraint was President Reagan's veto of the Textile Trade and Enforcement Act of 1985.

Termination of Special Protection

In terms of end-games, the 31 cases can be divided into three broad categories. The first and largest category, covering some 22 cases, includes cases that were either ongoing in 1985, or, at an earlier date, had been rolled over into another phase of protection (the textile and apparel, and carbon steel cases).

---

8. This point was made by Alexander W. Sierck, law offices of Beveridge and Diamond, in a private letter, January 26, 1986.

The second category, covering four cases, includes situations where special protection was terminated because of a cyclical revival in demand and an upsurge in product prices. This description applies to Carbon Steel: Phase I (the 1974 revival); Ball Bearings (the 1978 revival); Petroleum (tighter markets in the early 1970s, even before the 1973 oil shock); and Lead and Zinc (Vietnam War demand in the mid-1960s).

The third category, covering six instances of special protection,[9] includes cases where protection was terminated following adjustment—involving some combination of downsizing, product shifts, and modernization.

This categorization of cases suggests that, while adjustment occasionally points to the end of special protection, in far more cases protection endures indefinitely, or is brought to an end only by the happenstance of cyclical revival.

Characteristics of Special Protection

Special protection has several characteristics that deserve comment: the widespread use of quantitative restraints; the duration and review of protection; the costs to consumers and the efficiency loss to the nation; and the extent of adjustment during the life of trade restraints.

THE RISE OF QUANTITATIVE RESTRAINTS

In the postwar period, high tariffs have infrequently been used to inaugurate new cases of special protection.[10] Instead, special protection—especially in big cases—has usually entailed quantitative restraints (QRs), ranging from voluntary restraint agreements (VRAs), in which the restraints are imposed by the foreign country, to orderly marketing agreements (OMAs), in which

---

9. Specialty Steel is counted both as a case where protection was terminated in 1980 and, after being revived in 1983, as an ongoing case of protection.

10. New instances of special protection implemented with duties have largely been confined to escape clause cases. Significant escape clause cases, in terms of trade coverage, include Ceramic Articles (1972); Ball Bearings (1974); CB Radios (1978); Bolts, Nuts, and Large Screws (1979); Prepared Mushrooms (1980); and Motorcycles (1983). Smaller escape clause cases are listed in table 4.1.

restraints are monitored by the United States, to global and bilateral quotas in which the US Customs Service allows only fixed quantities to enter the United States.[11]

The use of QRs rather than high tariffs to restrain imports answers a strong preference of both domestic producers and foreign exporters. Domestic producers prefer QRs for three reasons: first, their share of the domestic market is more certain; second, domestic prices are less variable since fluctuations in foreign supply conditions do not so greatly affect quantities offered for sale in the US market; third, for a given degree of political "clout," the domestic industry can secure more protection through quantitative restraints than through tariffs, since the American public seems to understand the price-raising impact of tariffs but does not fully appreciate the effect of QRs on prices.

Foreign exporters prefer quantitative restraints for somewhat different reasons, and their reasons vary depending on whether they are traditional suppliers or new entrants to the US market. In the postwar period, most QRs have been selective: "well-behaved" exporting countries that are not perceived to be disrupting the domestic market are usually exempt from control. For this reason, traditional suppliers prefer QRs. They need not cut back their own exports; moreover, restrictions on third-country competitors may improve price levels in the US market and preserve their own shares of the US market.

By contrast, the foreign exporters that are affected—normally the "aggressive" new entrants—may prefer QRs to tariffs because QRs are customarily implemented in a way that confers valuable scarcity rents on the restrained exporters. Rents are created by artificial scarcity in the US market. These rents devolve on restrained exporters because quotas are allocated to foreign governments which in turn distribute the rights to established firms.[12] Both the United States and foreign exporters view this means of allocating quota rights as a method of payment to compensate restrained suppliers for

---

11. Unilateral quantitative restrictions made a "modern" appearance as early as 1463 when the British Parliament imposed a zero quota on a range of manufactured articles. By contrast, "voluntary" restraints on exports, negotiated between governments and implemented by the supplying country, date from US policy initiatives in the 1930s, first spawned by the National Industrial Recovery Act (Metzger 1971b, pp. 167–70).

12. The United States almost never auctions quota rights and seldom allocates them to US importers or producers—two methods of distribution that would deprive foreign suppliers of the scarcity rents. However, Australia, New Zealand, Brazil, the United Kingdom, and other countries have experimented with these alternative approaches.

their reduced export volumes.[13] This trade-off between volume and price makes QRs far more palatable than tariffs.

DURATION AND REVIEW

Cases of special protection vary widely in terms of the duration of protection and the frequency of review. At one extreme are instances of short-term relief lasting five years or less, exemplifed by Carbon Steel: Phase I, Nonrubber Footwear, Televisions, possibly Automobiles,[14] and (probably) Motorcycles. In these instances, relief was only designed to provide "breathing room." Restrictive measures were subject to periodic review, either by the explicit terms of the escape clause (Nonrubber Footwear; Televisions; Motorcycles; and numerous other cases) or by presidential plan (Carbon Steel: Phase I; Automobiles).

At the other extreme are protective measures designed to insulate the domestic industry from foreign competition for an extended period. "Indefinite protection" describes most of the high tariffs still standing from the Tariff Acts of 1922 and 1930. Other instances include the maritime laws (dating from 1789), the manufacturing clause in the US copyright law (dating from 1891), and the Magnuson Fisheries Act (dating from 1977).

Between these two extremes are cases in which constrained presidential review is permitted by statute. Section 22 of the Agricultural Adjustment Act of 1933 gives the Secretary of Agriculture authority to review sugar, dairy, peanut, and other agricultural quotas—subject always to the watchful eye of the domestic industries and their powerful congressional allies. Not surprisingly, sugar imports have been controlled since 1934 (with brief interludes during periods of soaring prices, in World War II and the mid-1970s), while dairy and peanuts imports have been limited since 1953. Similarly, section 204 of the Agricultural Act of 1956 nominally allows the President great flexibility in setting textile and apparel quotas—but in fact every decision is carefully monitored by Congress and the industry.

---

13. This point was first recognized in Bergsten (1975b, ch. 15).

14. The US–Japanese "voluntary" restraint agreement on automobile imports was replaced, in April 1985, by a voluntary export restraint system designed solely by the Japanese government, but implemented largely in response to congressional resolutions. Thus, trade restraints on automobiles remain in place.

PRICE, IMPORT, AND EMPLOYMENT EFFECTS

The last four columns of table 2.1 give rough estimates of the tariff or tariff equivalent of trade restraints, the induced increase in the price of domestically produced competing goods, the induced decrease in imports, and the induced increase in production jobs (or agricultural acreage or livestock). Much could be said about these estimates, but we shall confine our comments to a few highlights.

Tariff-equivalent rates of protection range from about 10 percent for automobiles and fisheries to nearly 100 percent for dairy products and petroleum. Most cases fall in the 15 percent to 40 percent bracket. The impact on prices charged by the domestic industry is a matter of controversy. In our judgment (which largely reflects the findings of other scholars), the "coefficient of price response" (the ratio of induced increase in the domestic price to the tariff-equivalent rate of protection) usually lies in the range of 0.3 to 0.5. Only for standardized commodities, such as orange juice and textiles, do we assign coefficients as high as 0.7 to 0.9. The coefficients of price response are almost always less than 1.0 because imported and domestic commodities are imperfect substitutes (both in product characteristics and in channels of distribution) and because the domestic industry is often an oligopoly with sticky price behavior.

Estimates for the induced decreases in imports are dominated by a few large cases: Textiles and Apparel; Carbon Steel; Automobiles; Maritime; Sugar; Dairy Products; Meat; and Petroleum. In big cases, imports are often reduced by $5 billion or more.

Estimates for induced increases in production jobs are dominated by the same cases, with the addition of four others: Book Manufacturing; Rubber Footwear; Nonrubber Footwear; and Fisheries. Apart from Textiles and Apparel, estimates of production jobs "saved" are decidedly small. Seldom do the figures exceed 10,000 workers. The estimates of jobs saved do not, however, include white collar employees, workers in ancillary industry (for example, workers making tires for automobiles), or retail and service employees in the immediate locality. On the other hand, the estimates make no allowance for the fact that higher costs in the protected industry undermine competitiveness in industries that use protected goods as inputs, or for the fact that higher prices erode real consumer purchasing power. All in all, the estimates in table 2.1 of jobs saved probably exaggerate the economy-wide employment induced by special protection.

COSTS OF SPECIAL PROTECTION

Table 2.2 presents estimates of the cost of special protection expressed both in terms of the total annual cost to consumers and in terms of the annual cost to consumers per production job "saved" (or per acre or head of livestock "saved"). Table 2.2 also gives estimates of the gains enjoyed by producers, both total and per job in the industry (or per acre or head of livestock). In addition, table 2.2 records estimates of the gains to foreigners, tariff revenues, and the efficiency losses to the economy.

Costs to consumers of special protection are huge. These costs represent a giant off-budget transfer from consumers on the one hand to producers and importers on the other. In Phase III of Textiles and Apparel the costs are running about $27.0 billion a year (the Textile Trade and Enforcement Act of 1985, vetoed by President Reagan in December 1985, would have added greatly to these costs); in Phase III of Carbon Steel, the costs in 1984 were about $6.8 billion; in Automobiles, about $5.8 billion; in Dairy Products, about $5.5 billion; and in most other ongoing cases the amounts exceed $100 million annually. All told, in 1984, the costs to consumers of currently ongoing special protection cases exceeded $50 billion (table 2.4).

Against these total costs, the production jobs "saved" in the affected industries are, on the whole, rather modest. By far the largest jobs-saved number is in Textiles and Apparel (640,000); followed by Automobiles (38,000), Fisheries (27,000), and Dairy (25,000). As a consequence, costs per production job saved are quite large, usually in the range of $20,000 to $100,000 per year, and often exceed $150,000. The fact that costs to consumers per production job saved are so high underpins the strategy for an alternative approach that would liberally compensate departing workers for moving to new industries and new locations, or taking early retirement.

Gains to producers averaged over all jobs are usually in the $4,000 to $20,000 a year range—a significant fraction of earnings per worker. In exceptional cases, such as Orange Juice and Petroleum, the calculated gains per worker substantially exceeded the annual wage bill per worker.

When trade restraints are imposed either through tariffs or through outright exclusion from the US market (as in Book Manufacturing and Maritime), foreign exporters gain nothing from the apparatus of protection. On the other hand, when quotas are assigned to foreign suppliers, the gains to foreign exporters can be handsome. For example, restraints imposed in Phase III of

Carbon Steel probably enrich foreign suppliers to the extent of about $2.0 billion annually.

The last column of table 2.2 cites efficiency losses to the economy. These are, of course, much smaller than costs to the consumer, since most of the consumer costs are reflected in higher producer incomes. Only in large cases do efficiency losses exceed $1.0 billion annually. On the other hand, a relatively small efficiency loss can be viewed as the functional equivalent of a much larger capital investment. Historically, the real rate of return to capital investment in the US economy is under 5 percent annually. Thus, an efficiency loss of "only" $330 million annually inflicted on the economy by steel import restraints (Carbon Steel: Phase III) represents the functional equivalent of at least $6.6 billion of capital investment denied the US economy.

ADJUSTMENT DURING SPECIAL PROTECTION

Table 2.3 summarizes the adjustment experience during episodes of special protection. The outstanding feature of this summary is that a great deal of downward adjustment does in fact take place, both in concluded cases and in ongoing cases.

In terms of labor-force adjustment, the number of production jobs almost always dropped during the episodes. Carbon steel employment has declined by over 10 percent per year since 1980; the rubber footwear, glassware, maritime, orange juice, and automobile industries have shed labor at rates in excess of 4 percent annually. Textile and apparel employment has dropped by about 1.6 percent annually since 1980. These rates of labor adjustment represent a signal accomplishment in an economy that has enjoyed nonagricultural employment growth of almost 3 percent a year since 1975. Likewise, the acreage or livestock in protected agricultural sectors generally falls. Even sugar acreage has dropped by more than 2 percent annually since 1973.

At the same time, the import share of the domestic market has usually been allowed to rise, if at constrained rates. Typically, the market share increase ranges from 0.5 percentage points to as much as 3 percentage points annually. Again, these are significant figures, considering that the overall penetration of foreign goods in the US market rose only 0.3 percentage points annually, from 5.5 percent to 10.0 percent between 1970 and 1985.

TABLE 2.2 Distribution of costs and benefits from special protection

Case	Cost of restraints to consumers		Gain from restraints to producers		Welfare costs of restraints		
	Totals (million dollars)	Per job saved[a] (dollars)	Totals (million dollars)	Per job[a] (dollars)	Gain to foreigners (million dollars)	Tariff revenue (million dollars)	Efficiency loss (million dollars)
Manufacturing							
M-1 Book Manufacturing	500	100,000	305	9,000	neg.	0	29
M-2 Benzenoid Chemicals	2,650	over 1 million	2,250	37,000	neg.	252	14
M-3 Glassware	200	200,000	130	11,000	neg.	54	13
M-4 Rubber Footwear	230	30,000	90	6,400	neg.	139	33
M-5 Ceramic Articles	95	47,500	25	3,100	neg.	69	6
M-6 Ceramic Tiles	116	135,000	62	10,000	neg.	55	11
M-7 Orange Juice	525	240,000	390	90,000	neg.	128	130
M-8 Canned Tuna	91	76,000	74	5,500	7	10	4
M-9 Textiles and Apparel: Phase I	9,400	22,000	8,700	4,000	neg.	1,158	1,100
M-10 Textiles and Apparel: Phase II	20,000	37,000	18,000	8,700	350	2,143	3,100
M-11 Textiles and Apparel: Phase III	27,000	42,000	22,000	11,100	1,800	2,535	4,850
M-12 Carbon Steel: Phase I	1,970	240,000	1,330	3,400	330	290	50
M-13 Carbon Steel: Phase II	4,350	620,000	2,770	9,700	930	556	120
M-14 Carbon Steel: Phase III	6,800	750,000	3,800	22,000	2,000	560	330
M-15 Ball Bearings	45	90,000	21	500	neg.	18	neg.

M-16 Specialty Steel	520	1,000,000	420	60,000	50	32	30
M-17 Nonrubber Footwear	700	55,000	250	2,000	220	262	16
M-18 Color Televisions	420	420,000	190	9,000	140	77	7
M-19 CB Radios	55	93,000	14	6,400	neg.	32	5
M-20 Bolts, Nuts, Large Screws	110	550,000	60	5,500	neg.	16	1
M-21 Prepared Mushrooms	35	117,000	13	4,300	neg.	25	0.8
M-22 Automobiles	5,800	105,000	2,600	4,300	2,200	790	200
M-23 Motorcycles	104	150,000	67	20,000	neg.	21	17
Services							
S-1 Maritime Industries	3,000	270,000	2,000	130,000	neg.	10[b]	1,000
Agriculture and Fisheries							
A-1 Sugar	930	60,000 690/acre	550	27,000 180/acre	410	5	130
A-2 Dairy Products	5,500	220,000 1,800/cow	5,000	53,000 450/cow	250	34	1,370
A-3 Peanuts	170	1,000/acre	170	120/acre	neg.	9	14
A-4 Meat	1,800	160,000 225/head	1,600	9,500 20/head	135	44	145
A-5 Fish	560	21,000	200	900	170	177	15
Mining							
E-1 Petroleum	6,900	160,000	4,800	61,500	2,000[c]	70	3,000
E-2 Lead and Zinc	67	30,000	46	2,300	4	11	5

Neg. Negligible.

a. Unless otherwise specified, figures are per worker.

b. Estimated duties collected on ship repairs performed abroad.

c. In this case, because of the way the quotas were allocated, the gains to importers accrued to domestic refiners rather than foreign exporters.

TABLE 2.3 **Adjustment during special protection**[a]

	Employment[b]			Import share		
Case	Pre-restraint (thousands)	Post-restraint (thousands)	Annual change (percentage)	Pre-restraint (percentage)	Post-restraint (percentage)	Annual change (percentage points)
Manufacturing						
M–1 Book Manufacturing	37 (1979)	33 (1984)	–2.2	10.0 (1979)	19.5 (1984)	1.9
M–2 Benzenoid Chemicals	70 (1978)	61 (1984)	–2.1	1.0 (1978)	1.6 (1984)	0.1
M–3 Glassware	15 (1978)	12 (1983)	–4.0	10.5 (1978)	21.6 (1983)	2.2
M–4 Rubber Footwear	22 (1975)	14 (1983)	–4.5	39.8 (1975)	62.4 (1983)	2.8
M–5 Ceramic Articles	10 (1978)	8 (1984)	–3.3	50.7 (1976)	66.0 (1984)	1.9
M–6 Ceramic Tiles	7 (1972)	6 (1984)	–1.2	33.2 (1976)	57.9 (1984)	3.1
M–7 Orange Juice	5 (1978)	4 (1983)	–4.0	16.2 (1979)	29.5 (1983)	2.7
M–8 Canned Tuna	15 (1979)	13 (1983)	–2.2	6.8 (1978)	17.9 (1983)	2.2
M–9 Textiles and Apparel: Phase I	2,137 (1955)	2,140 (1974)	0.0	6.3 (1960)	8.4 (1974)	0.2
M–10 Textiles and Apparel: Phase II	2,194 (1972)	2,067 (1981)	–0.6	9.6 (1972)	14.0 (1981)	0.5
M–11 Textiles and Apparel: Phase III	2,112 (1980)	1,980 (1984)	–1.6	12.1 (1980)	20.4 (1984)	2.1

M-12 Carbon Steel: Phase I	421 (1968)	339 (1975)	-2.8	16.7 (1968)	13.5 (1975)	-0.5
M-13 Carbon Steel: Phase II	337 (1977)	286 (1981)	-3.8	17.8 (1977)	21.8 (1982)	0.8
M-14 Carbon Steel: Phase III	292 (1980)	171 (1984)	-10.4	16.4 (1980)	26.7 (1984)	2.6
M-15 Ball Bearings	44 (1973)	43 (1979)	-0.4	23.7 (1973)	30.1 (1979)	1.1
M-16 Specialty Steel	16 (1975)	14 (1984)	-1.3	18.1 (1975)	16.8 (1984)	-0.1
M-17 Nonrubber Footwear	136 (1975)	122 (1982)	-1.5	41.3 (1975)	59.0 (1982)	2.5
M-18 Color Televisions	27 (1976)	21 (1982)	-3.7	38.5 (1979)	34.2 (1983)	-1.1
M-19 CB Radios	3 (1976)	neg. (1982)	-15.2	94.0 (1976)	97.0 (1983)	0.5
M-20 Bolts, Nuts, Large Screws	13 (1978)	10 (1982)	-5.3	40.9 (1978)	49.9 (1982)	2.3
M-21 Prepared Mushrooms	3 (1979)	3 (1982)	0.0	51.8 (1979)	62.4 (1984)	2.1
M-22 Automobiles	779 (1979)	605 (1984)	-4.5	28.3 (1979)	34.2 (1984)	1.2
M-23 Motorcycles	2 (1982)	3 (1984)	25.0	69.0 (1982)	31.0 (1984)	-19.0
Services						
S-1 Maritime Industries	37 (1970)	14 (1984)	-4.4	65.2 (1970)	62.3 (1983)	-0.2
Agriculture and Fisheries						
A-1 Sugar	29	20	-4.4	50.3	34.5	-1.6

TABLE 2.3 **Adjustment during special protection** (*continued*)[a]

	Employment[b]			Import share		
Case	Pre-restraint (thousands)	Post-restraint (thousands)	Annual change (percentage)	Pre-restraint (percentage)	Post-restraint (percentage)	Annual change (percentage points)
Agriculture and Fisheries						
A–1 Sugar	29	20	–4.4	50.3 (1974)	34.5 (1984)	–1.6
	2,300 (acres)	1,800 (acres)	–3.1			
A–2 Dairy Products	97	94	–0.6	4.5 (1978)	4.2 (1983)	–0.1
	10,900 (cows) (1978)	11,100 (cows) (1983)	0.4			
A–3 Peanuts	6	6	–1.2	neg.	neg.	neg.
	1,520 (acres) (1974)	1,410 (acres) (1983)	–0.8			
A–4 Meat	189	168	–0.6	3.6 (1964)	5.9 (1983)	0.1
	108,000 (head) (1963)	114,000 (head) (1983)	0.3			
A–5 Fish	173 (1976)	216 (1982)	4.1	62.5 (1976)	61.5 (1983)	–0.1
Mining						
E–1 Petroleum	140 (1954)	75 (1975)	–2.7	9.9 (1954)	25.8 (1975)	0.8
E–2 Lead and Zinc	28 (1957)	20 (1966)	–3.4	58.2 (1957)	37.6 (1966)	–2.3

Neg. Negligible.

a. In lengthy and ongoing cases, the pre- and post-restraint figures are actually the first and the last years of data that we included in the case.

b. Unless otherwise specified, figures refer to the number of production jobs in the industry.

Special protection as practiced in the United States cannot, for the most part, be faulted for freezing the status quo. Instead, it should be criticized for providing rather little assistance to workers and firms that are forced to depart the troubled industry; for imposing huge costs on consumers; for not promoting a smooth transition to the realities of international competition; and for engendering widespread opposition to trade liberalization.

Assessment of Special Protection

The US system of special protection is far from the worst system imaginable. Indeed, the system has several virtues. In the first place, a presidential policy of making slow and grudging concessions to troubled industries, coupled with less-than-watertight regimes of protection, allows a great deal of adjustment to take place. Before trade restraints are put in place, the industry usually sheds a substantial number of workers and concedes market share to imports. Even after restraints are in place, the import share of the market typically rises and employment continues to shrink.

Moreover, relief may turn out to be temporary. Despite the fears of skeptics and the hopes of industry, many instances of special protection do not ripen into a maritime story, a book printing story, or an apparel story. Although highly inefficient from an economic standpoint, the use of VRAs, OMAs, and other QRs minimizes international abrasion as long as quota rents are conferred on foreigners. Finally, special protection for problem industries has not so far precluded liberalization in other sectors of the economy, notably through seven rounds of GATT negotiations.

In short, the US system of special protection has its strong points. Scholars of the Bert Lance school might say, "If it ain't broke, don't fix it." Yet, while not completely "broke," the system has six conspicuous defects by comparison with a policy framework that would place greater stress on the original purposes of the GATT Article XIX escape clause—namely time-limited, degressive protection, applied on a most-favored-nation (MFN) basis, coupled with meaningful adjustment policies.

First, the trade coverage of special protection is growing. Table 2.4 gives summary statistics. The trade coverage (expressed in current dollars) in 1955 was $0.6 billion; in 1960, $3.4 billion; in 1970, $9.7 billion; in 1980, $28.9 billion; and in 1984, $67.6 billion. As a percentage of US imports, special protection tapered off after the end of petroleum restraints, but grew from 8 percent of imports in 1975 to 21 percent in 1984. The reduction of US

TABLE 2.4 **Special protection related to total trade**[a]

Year	Total US imports (billion dollars)	US imports covered by special protection — Annual average (million dollars)	US imports covered by special protection — Share of total imports (percentage)	Consumer cost of special protection[b] — Annual average (million dollars)	Consumer cost of special protection[b] — Share of total imports (percentage)	Induced decrease in imports — Annual average (million dollars)	Induced decrease in imports — Share of total imports (percentage)	Tariff equivalent of special protection (million dollars)	Tariff equivalent of special protection (percentage)	Division of tariff equivalent — Tariff revenue[c] (million dollars)	Division of tariff equivalent — Implied quota rents[d] (million dollars)	Relative wholesale prices[e] (1975 = 100)
1955	11.6	577	5	703	6	629	5	180	31	21	159	118.6
1960[f]	15.1	3,380	22	6,352	42	5,917	39	1,931	57	302	1,629	126.2
1965[f]	21.5	4,759	22	9,627	45	8,720	41	2,665	56	440	2,225	116.5
1970[f]	40.2	9,655	24	16,439	41	14,631	36	4,499	47	847	3,652	118.2
1975	99.3	7,894	8	13,117	13	12,424	12	2,202	28	1,375	827	100.0
1980	245.3	28,928	12	32,749	13	22,619	9	6,147	21	3,445	2,702	93.9
1984[g]	328.7	67,597	21	53,474	16	44,431	13	13,713	20	6,123	7,590	135.5

a. These figures do not include the maritime case (S–1) since the import statistics are not comparable with those in other cases.

b. The consumer cost for those years not included in the cases themselves and in which protection was ongoing, was derived by relating the current year cost to current year trade and adjusting the cost with the trade level of other years.

c. The tariff equivalent and tariff revenue were estimated by applying the rates in the case to all years in which the case was ongoing, even though some variation in tariff and quota levels undoubtedly occurred.

d. The quota rents were derived simply by subtracting the estimated tariff revenue from the dollar value of the tariff equivalent.

e. The figures for 1955 and 1960 are based on Helen B. Junz and Rudolf R. Rhomberg, "Prices and Export Performance of Industrial Countries, 1953–63," *IMF Staff Papers*, 12, no. 2 (July 1965): table 9, p. 269. The figures for 1965 to 1984 are based on the table, "Cost and Price Comparisons for Mfg." in IMF, *International Financial Statistics*.

f. The unusually high levels of protection and relative consumer costs in the years 1960, 1965, and 1970 are due to restricted petroleum imports which accounted for an average 42 percent of covered trade in those years.

g. Some of the figures are for 1983.

imports on account of special protection grew from $12.4 billion in 1975 to some $44.4 billion in 1984. The rise in special protection since 1980 is closely related to the appreciation of the dollar against major foreign currencies. Between 1980 and 1984, US wholesale prices rose, relative to the wholesale prices of its major trading partners expressed in US dollars (and therefore reflecting exchange rate changes), from an index level of 93.9 to an index level of 135.5 (table 2.4). In March 1985, the dollar began its long-awaited correction against foreign currencies, and, as this correction continues, much of the special protection witnessed in the mid-1980s should begin to erode. Nevertheless, it seems likely that a good part of the protective edifice will be preserved by industry-specific pressures.

Second, special protection is costly to consumers, both in total consumer costs and in consumer costs per production job "saved." Figures of $20,000 to $100,000 consumer costs per job-year saved are common, and figures above $150,000 occur all too often. These figures represent a high price for the goal usually announced—namely to preserve blue collar employment in the afflicted industry.

Third, special protection diverts scarce resources to America's least promising industries. Almost by definition, industries that need special protection are industries that have lost their competitive edge in the world economy. These industries do not draw on the comparative strength of the US labor force. They are industries in which foreign producers have acquired new technology that is as good, or better, than US technology.

Fourth, special protection is highly inequitable as between industries. Large industries with political clout—dairy, apparel, automobiles—are able to shake the US political system for massive benefits. Small industries with only regional influence—footwear, copper, CB radios—at best get escape clause relief and often get nothing. Unfairness may be a fact of political life, but it is not an attractive fact.

Fifth, special protection is associated with huge quota rents, largely accruing to foreign producers. In 1984, the figure was running at $7.6 billion annually. The creation and allocation of quota rents, together with the practice of allocating quotas according to historical market shares, serves to entrench established patterns of production, on a worldwide scale, rather than encourage adjustment to changing comparative advantage. For example, Europe rather than Korea continues as a major supplier of carbon steel to the US market.

Sixth, in recent years, special protection has come to impede new initiatives for trade liberalization. In the days when special protection was limited to sugar, dairy, cotton textiles, oil, and a few other products, it did not seriously interfere with the Kennedy Round of trade negotiations. Now that special protection has spread to autos, steel, most textiles, meat, and many other goods, it stands as a major obstacle to multilateral trade liberalization.

In light of these six shortcomings, and our reviews of labor adjustment and past policies, which appear in chapters 3 and 4, chapter 5 offers a new trade policy for troubled industries. The new policy calls for centralizing relief under a refurbished escape clause. The purpose of relief under the new plan, as under the existing escape clause, is to provide temporary ''breathing room'' for orderly adjustment, not to provide a facade for indefinite protection. Assured funding for adjustment purposes is built into the plan. Finally, the plan calls for interlocking adjustment obligations between the major trading powers within the framework of a new GATT Safeguards and Adjustment Code.

3 Labor Adjustment to Import Competition

Largely as a consequence of an overvalued dollar, the United States has experienced a massive deterioration in its manufactured goods trade balance, which dropped from a surplus of $17 billion in 1980 to a record deficit of over $110 billion in 1985.[1] Over the same period, US manufacturing employment fell from almost 21 million to 19.5 million workers. Even though overall US employment rose from 99 million in 1980 to 106 million in 1985, these events in the manufacturing sector exerted great pressure on US trade policy. A political connection is frequently drawn between import competition and unemployment, even though the economic connection is sometimes uncertain.[2]

Certain generalizations can be made about industries that are most affected by changing trade patterns. A review of about a dozen studies performed over the last decade suggests that trade-related dislocation is concentrated in textiles, apparel, leather products, steel, and electrical and electronic equipment (Mutti and Rosen 1986, table 23). These industries account for a quarter of US manufacturing employment. Most of these industries also appear in a Bureau of Labor Statistics list of sectors expected to experience employment loss between 1979 and 1990 (Personick 1983, pp. 30–32). Not surprisingly, these same industries have often sought trade relief. Table 3.1 presents data on the distribution by industry of escape clause relief cases. Five industries consistently identified as trade-impacted represent over 30 percent of the

---

1. Much of the deterioration in the US trade account can be explained by the appreciation of the dollar during the first half of the 1980s and its sustained overvaluation through 1985 (Marris 1985).

2. The introduction to this chapter, together with sections 1, 2, and 4, are adapted from Mutti and Rosen (1986) and Orr (1986).

TABLE 3.1   **Distribution of import relief cases and injury determinations by industry, 1975–84**

Industry	Cases filed before ITC	Injury determination	Affirmative presidential action
Food products	11	6	3
Tobacco	1	0	0
Apparel	3	1	1
Lumber and wood products	1	1	1
Chemicals	1	1	0
Rubber and plastics	2	1	1
Leather products	3	2	2
Stone, clay, and glass products	1	1	1
Primary metals	10	6	3
Fabricated metals	10	6	2
Electrical and electronic equipment	2	2	2
Transportation equipment	3	1	1
Miscellaneous manufacturing	3	1	0
Total manufacturing	51	29	17

Source: Mutti and Rosen 1986.

escape clause cases brought between 1975 and 1984, and some 40 percent of the injury determinations.[3]

Adjustment Costs in the Labor Market

Successful labor market adjustment is harder to achieve than industry adjustment since workers are often unable to adjust as quickly as firms. Substantial adjustment costs borne by workers are often translated into

---

3. The 40 percent figure includes split-vote injury determinations by the USITC. Textiles and apparel are underrepresented in the escape clause list because these two industries are largely protected by the Multi-Fiber Arrangement (MFA). Specialized industries within the textile and apparel sector that experience import pressures are usually accommodated in subsequent negotiations of bilateral agreements under the MFA.

political pressure, which in turn leads to special protection. Labor adjustment costs can be classified under three major headings:

- income losses, both temporary and permanent

- asset losses, including nonfinancial "assets" such as employment benefits

- the physical and psychological impact of job loss.

Some research has been done on estimating income losses, but there is little empirical work on the other two forms of adjustment cost.

Estimates suggest that permanently displaced workers experience a loss of between 1 percent and 47 percent in average annual earnings during the first two years after layoff, depending on the industry affected. The experience of most workers improves after four years, with workers experiencing between an 11 percent gain and an 18 percent loss in earnings. However, trade-impacted workers tend to be older, less educated, female, and minorities (Aho and Orr 1981, pp. 29–34). These workers may be less able to find alternative employment than the "average" displaced worker.

Asset losses of displaced workers can be separated into financial and nonfinancial losses. Financial losses include pension losses (if a worker is not vested), depleted personal savings, and costs of geographical relocation. Workers who choose to move may be forced to sell their houses in markets that are depressed because of severe dislocation within the entire community. The severity of this cost may explain workers' resistance to relocating.

The principal nonfinancial asset cost is the loss of health and pension benefits. The lapse in health insurance policies not only affects workers during unemployment, but also affects their subsequent coverage. In most cases, health insurance still does not cover preexisting conditions.[4]

It is almost impossible to measure the physical and psychological impact of economic dislocation. A survey of the unemployed in Michigan, however,

---

4. For example, if a worker develops hypertension during the period between jobs when he is not covered by health insurance, his new policy may not be obligated to cover medical expenses for that illness. However, some firms extend the insurance coverage of their workers for several months after separation and some plans allow workers to contribute to their policies after separation. During the peak of the 1981–82 recession, state and federal legislation was enacted to help workers either maintain their existing insurance policies or acquire alternative health insurance coverage. BLS reports that three-quarters of the displaced workers surveyed had health insurance on their original jobs. The majority of the workers still looking for work in January 1984 were without health insurance (US Department of Labor 1985).

found that twice as many respondents reported that their health had gotten worse since job termination compared with those whose health had improved.

The Bureau of Labor Statistics recently surveyed 11.5 million workers who lost their jobs due to plant closings or employment cutbacks between January 1979 and January 1984 (US Department of Labor 1985). Nearly half of those surveyed, some 5.1 million workers, worked at least three years on their jobs prior to layoff. Two-thirds of the workers were reemployed, one-quarter of the workers were still looking for jobs, and the remaining workers had left the labor force by January 1984.

More than half of the displaced workers who were reemployed in January 1984 took jobs in industries *other* than those in which they were originally employed. Earnings losses varied among workers. Workers originally employed in durable goods manufacturing experienced a 21 percent drop in wages while workers originally employed in nondurable goods manufacturing experienced almost no reduction in wages. Only 13 percent of the dislocated workers moved to a different city or county to locate a new job.

The regional concentration of trade-impacted industries (such as autos in Michigan, textiles and footwear in New England, and steel in the mid-Atlantic states) compounds the adjustment costs borne by workers. Since the average wage in manufacturing exceeds the average wage in the economy by 25 percent, the transition to another manufacturing job is generally easier than the transition to a service job. But with the net decline in manufacturing employment throughout the economy, many workers are forced to take service jobs.

In response to inevitable, if unwelcome, pressures for adjustment in a changing economy, the United States has devised a two-tiered approach to displaced workers. The first tier consists of the traditional unemployment insurance (UI) programs operated by individual states. Nearly 5 million employers contribute taxes to finance the state portion of the program. These programs provide all eligible unemployed workers with weekly benefits to replace lost earnings and an array of services to assist the unemployed in getting new jobs. In all, about 88 million workers, or 97 percent of all wage and salary workers, are covered by the UI system. In fiscal 1982, a year of high unemployment, $21.3 billion in unemployment compensation and related benefits was paid to 11.4 million unemployed workers.

Most states now pay benefits for 26 weeks. Extended benefits up to an additional 13 weeks are triggered in states that experience very high unemployment, with the cost shared 50–50 between the states and the federal government. In periods of recession, the federal government has extended benefits for longer durations.

A second tier of programs attempts to answer the problems of specific displaced workers. The second tier programs are small in a national context. They include Trade Adjustment Assistance (TAA), the Job Training Partnership Act (JTPA), and several demonstration projects.

Trade Adjustment Assistance

Trade adjustment programs[5] fall into the category of "second-best" policy approaches. Ideally, government should foster adjustment to economic change across-the-board, whether the impetus comes from inside or outside national borders. But comprehensive adjustment policies seem well beyond the reach of the US government. In their absence, firms and workers threatened by international competition press government to impose trade barriers. Trade adjustment programs are a useful means of responding to these pressures. Hence the persistence of such programs on the American policy scene.

ADJUSTMENT ASSISTANCE AS AN ALTERNATIVE TO PROTECTION

Trade adjustment assistance first became a component of American trade policy through its incorporation in the Trade Expansion Act of 1962. The purpose was to offer a constructive alternative to trade protection, by aiding industry and worker efforts to cope with import competition through retraining, reequipment, and new products. But the program's effectiveness was limited by the broader character of the postwar American trade policy regime, as a brief recounting of the rise and fall of TAA makes clear.

David McDonald of the United Steelworkers, a member of the Randall Commission advising Congress and President Dwight D. Eisenhower on future trade policy, proposed in 1953 a program of direct federal aid to firms, communities, and workers injured by imports. The Commission voted 16 to 1 against the idea, but gave it mention in the report. Democratic senators picked the idea up: doctrinally, it was a way to be economically activist at home while remaining liberal internationally; politically, it was a way to

---

5. This section is adapted from Destler (1986).

offer something to those hurt by imports while steering clear of "protectionism."

When, in 1961, one of those senators became President, TAA became a natural component of his Trade Expansion Act. TAA helped retain big labor's support for liberal trade, by offering its leaders a rationale for backing a policy that was becoming increasingly controversial among the rank and file. And its broad shape and purpose were consistent with other nontrade adjustment programs the Kennedy administration was inaugurating or expanding, such as area redevelopment and manpower retraining.

Judging from the contemporary debate, the TAA program was pretty big. The most comprehensive trade policymaking study of this period declared it "a proposal which, if adopted, could destroy the political basis of protectionism by giving the injured a way out."[6] The authors saw it as one of *the* great, forward-looking trade ideas of the period, a way of fostering change, allowing society as a whole to reap the benefits of trade while helping those whose interests were being sacrificed for the broader public good. Opponents assigned it comparable importance. Two Republican critics denounced its "mere insertion" in the Randall Commission report as reflecting "a dangerous sentiment" in favor of what was, to them, socialistic intervention in private business.

Controversial and big it was in concept: it survived the Ways and Means Committee markup by a single vote. But in practice, the actual Kennedy program proved very small. To repeat the oft-cited numbers, not a single trade-displaced worker actually got aid in the years through fiscal year 1969, and only 48,314 won benefits through 1974. The proximate reason was that the eligibility criteria were too stringently drawn. Under section 302 of the Trade Expansion Act of 1962, firms and workers faced a triple burden of proof: they had to demonstrate: (1) serious injury (meaning significant unemployment), (2) caused by imports, (3) resulting from specific US "concessions granted under trade agreements." The larger reason was the inconsistency of the TAA concept with the way American trade policy actually operated during this period. US trade laws acted, in practice, *not* to *address* the specific impact of imports on the domestic economy, but to *finesse* them.

---

6. See Bauer, de Sola Pool, and Dexter (1972, p. 43). Similarly, Preeg (1970, p. 48) labeled TAA a "radical innovation."

And it was not just workers who could not qualify for trade benefits. From 1963 to 1974, for example, the US Tariff Commission found injury justifying trade relief in only 4 of 30 escape clause cases presented by import-competing firms.

Those few import-threatened industries that had political clout went around such procedures and got their own help through direct executive or congressional action: textiles and apparel were the prime example, together with agricultural commodities like sugar and dairy products. And their goal was, naturally enough, the opposite of adjustment: they wanted much larger domestic market shares than open trade would have allowed.

Contemporary political alignments in the 1960s worked to finesse trade adjustment problems. Republicans, from whose ranks came most protectionists of the period, were biased against all forms of direct government aid to business or labor. Democrats, who initiated the TAA program, were not yet facing severe protectionist pressure from labor so they lacked an overwhelming incentive to make sure that adjustment assistance was working. And those legislators (and executive officials) strongly interested in labor adjustment and "structural" unemployment gave their priority to economy-wide programs like the Manpower Development and Training Act (MDTA), which was also initiated by President John F. Kennedy and Congress in 1962.

In the short run, the limited implementation of TAA and the escape clause generated little political reaction. The nation was still prospering at home and preeminent in the world. The United States enjoyed continuing growth, low trade exposure, and a rather stable trade environment. Exchange rates were fixed. American firms faced resurgent competition from the new European Community, but they had yet to confront the Japan of the 1970s or its East Asian emulators.

By 1973, when the Nixon administration sought authority for a new trade negotiating round, the general economic conditions had changed, specifically the overvaluation of the dollar during this period, resulting in growing protectionist pressure. Congress responded by seeking to make the quasi-judicial remedies *real*. Still, protection was not to be the norm, as the labor-backed Burke-Hartke bill of 1971 proposed, but the exception. It was not to be legislated directly by Congress, but administered through regulatory procedures and institutions through which trade-impacted interests would have to argue their cases.

As part of this broader effort to revive the trade remedy laws, Congress liberalized access to TAA—new workers and firms could qualify if increased imports "contributed importantly" to unemployment. Ways and Means Democrats led in this effort. They were resisted by the administration's "economic czar," Treasury Secretary George P. Shultz, who opposed a separate trade adjustment program on principle, preferring comprehensive reform of the unemployment compensation system. Nor could TAA any longer be used to buy labor support. In fact, the AFL–CIO now opposed trade liberalization and characterized TAA as "burial insurance," though big labor nonetheless wanted to improve worker access to the program and expand worker benefits. But the legislators saw TAA as substantively desirable and politically useful—as preferable to import restrictions, and as something they could give labor. They worked with the Special Trade Representative-led executive branch to draft a compromise which Shultz bought onto, reluctantly, as a price for House action on a bill broadly to his liking.

Now the program really began to be used: in fiscal years 1977 through 1979, over 100,000 workers a year received from $148 million to $265 million in annual benefits. TAA had established, at last, a marginal political utility to executive branch trade leaders and to legislators. In the policy community, its prime constituency was liberal traders. Most of those concerned with broader problems of adjustment and structural unemployment continued to have reservations about the equity and efficiency of special trade-related programs. Nevertheless, the trade adjustment program was now playing at least three distinct roles in support of liberal American trade policies.

TAA was, first of all, a *coalition-builder for major trade legislation*. The initiation, expansion, and refinement of the program clearly broadened the political base for the trade acts of 1962 and 1974.

Second, it was a *nonprotectionist option for presidents*. Once an import issue was pressed on them by the legal or political process, TAA was something presidents could give a trade-afflicted industry other than tariffs or quotas. Gerald R. Ford could "expedite adjustment assistance" for footwear in 1976, and Jimmy Carter could do the same for autos in 1980. Neither industry was satisfied, but it was better than nothing.

Third, the distribution of TAA benefits could serve as a *diluter of discontent*. Displaced workers in import-competing industries would not be happy with it; they wanted their old jobs back, not higher unemployment compensation and training opportunities. Nevertheless, they were less insistent in seeking protection when their incomes were being maintained at close to accustomed levels.

But the last of these uses, the partial buying-off of labor, cost the program in much more than dollars. With a large number of unemployed auto workers receiving trade adjustment money for the first time, benefit payments increased sixfold between fiscal years 1979 and 1980. At this very time, evaluation studies were casting doubt on the program's equity and efficiency. The studies offered "very little support for the notion that in general trade-displaced workers are very different from other displaced workers," thus undercutting the rationale for a separate program. They offered little support also for "the notion that TAA has encouraged much labor market mobility" (Aho and Bayard 1984b, pp. 30, 36, 47).

So the program became a fat and vulnerable target for Ronald Reagan and David A. Stockman as they searched for government expenditures to slash. TAA's defenders were disillusioned. In 1981, Congressman Sam M. Gibbons (D-Fla.), one of the champions of the program's reform in 1974, had just become Chairman of the House Ways and Means Subcommittee on Trade, but he was now inclined to write the program off as a well-intentioned mistake. Its remaining defenders were no match for a new administration in its strongest year. The program found its benefit levels cut back sharply—to those of regular unemployment insurance—in the omnibus budget legislation.

The 1981 experience exposed two serious TAA weaknesses. First, as Aho and Bayard (1984b) have explained, it has three goals which compete in practice: equity (as among workers), efficiency (in promoting adjustment), and political efficacy (in deflecting protectionist pressures). It was doing useful service when judged by the third criterion, but it was hard to defend *as a program* if found wanting on the first two. (Ironically, political effectiveness is not always a strong argument within the political arena![7]) Second, attachment to the pressure-diverting function was strongest among those giving priority to trade policy. They could, in general, keep the upper hand on trade bills, but once the decision moved to another political arena— one involving overall public spending—they could not.

Since 1981, TAA has limped along, with a two-year extension in 1983. The program was to expire on September 30, 1985, but was temporarily extended, along with all other government programs, to November 15, and again to December 19, 1985. In the meantime, the Reagan administration decided not to approve any extension of the program. In the final days of 1985, Congress extended only the training and relocation components of

---

7. See, for example, a scathing editorial in *The Washington Post*, a staunch "free-trade" newspaper, happily describing the TAA program as "a shadow of its former swollen self," questioning why "trade-affected workers [should] be so favored," and urging that the program be allowed to die ("Buying Off Protectionism," 14 September 1983, p. A20).

TAA, stopping *all* cash payments. The Labor Department continues to certify workers, but only for noncash benefits.

With the near-demise of TAA, the trade policymaking system has lost what had been in practice a marginal, but intermittently useful, protection-combating instrument. By the early 1980s, however, a different approach to adjustment was gaining support. This one saw adjustment steps as an adjunct to, and a *quid pro quo* for, protection, not an alternative.

ADJUSTMENT CONDITIONS AS A COMPLEMENT TO PROTECTION

Proposals for adjustment conditions linked to trade protection represent a sharp departure from the postwar American trade policymaking tradition. They assume that some sort of import relief is likely to prove the norm for industries facing strong foreign competition. To avert the worst consequences of trade relief, they would link it to adoption of sector-specific adjustment programs. This could fall well short of a full-fledged industrial policy, but it nonetheless calls for significant government involvement in decisions traditionally reserved to private enterprise.

President Jimmy Carter's Treasury Department responded to steel industry pressure by developing the trigger price mechanism (TPM). Beyond its primary goal of countering dumped foreign steel, the TPM had the added objective of discouraging US firms from raising prices. Congress used Chrysler's need for loan guarantees to force a packet of cost-cutting concessions by management and labor. Charles L. Schultze, the anti-protectionist chairman of Carter's Council of Economic Advisers, urged that, if the auto industry was granted trade relief, it should be conditioned on similar industry-labor commitments.

The Reagan administration did not take this course on autos, but it acted favorably on the escape clause case brought by the Harley-Davidson motor-cycle company in 1983. In that case, the firm took the initiative in offering adjustment commitments tied to temporary trade relief. When the USITC found injury to carbon steel producers and recommended trade relief in July 1984, it urged that protection be linked to industry adjustment plans. If subsequent reviews "do not reveal meaningful efforts to adjust by all involved in the steel industry," said Commissioner David Rohr, who wrote the majority opinion, "the relief should be terminated."[8] Following up this theme, the

---

8. *Wall Street Journal*, 12 July 1984, p. 2.

Trade and Tariff Act of 1984 called on the steel industry to reinvest its cash flow in the steel industry in return for negotiated steel quotas.

Not surprisingly, this sort of linkage became a standard feature of trade policy documents. It was particularly popular among Democrats, who were inclined toward economic intervention, subject to heavy labor pressure on trade, skeptical of business, and not wishing to come across as out-and-out protectionists.[9] In the trade business, the new buzz word was "conditionality." There was something in it for almost everybody. It was a way to advocate restrictions without seeming to be in industry's pocket: firms and workers would pay a price through adjustment sacrifices. For liberal traders it was a way to make the best of a bad thing; perhaps it might even discourage future claims if it became clear that trade relief would not come free.

Can the conditionality approach be applied broadly? Would it serve adjustment aims? What support and what opposition might it generate? To explore these questions requires a closer look at specific proposals. The most prominent is a bill (S 1863) introduced, originally in 1983, then again in 1985 as part of the Republican-sponsored Trade Enhancement Act of 1985, by Senator John Heinz (R-Pa.). This bill would offer an import-injured industry a new trade-relief option. The price would be the development and implementation of a joint management-labor adjustment plan.

Upon petitioning the USITC for relief, the industry could request the creation of an "adjustment plan development group" to devise a strategy for dealing with the industry's problems. The group would consist of industry and labor representatives, as well as advisers from the US Trade Representative (USTR), the Departments of Commerce and Labor, and other agencies found appropriate by USTR. The plan could include such steps as reductions in capacity, technological improvements, investment changes, improvements in productivity or management, cost reductions, and relief from government regulations. Neither the development nor the implementation of the plan would "be treated as a violation of any Federal or State antitrust law."

The group would submit the plan to the petitioners three months into the USITC injury investigation, and the petitioners in turn would decide whether to submit the plan to the USITC. The USITC then would submit this plan along with its remedy recommendation to the President. If the President chose not to grant the relief, he would have to obtain congressional approval for alternative action; otherwise the USITC remedy would take effect. The

9. The 1984 Democratic Party platform pledged that, "If temporary trade relief is granted, the quid pro quo for relief will be a realistic, hardheaded modernization plan which will restore competitiveness involving commitments by all affected parties."

President could not, as under the present escape clause, deny the relief (or alter its form) in the name of the broader "national economic interest of the United States." Elements of the plan requiring legislation would be considered under the "fast track" procedures of the Trade Act.[10]

The inducement for industry participation in the Heinz scheme is the prospect of more certain import relief. The lack of presidential discretion creates a high probability that some form of relief would be granted.

But in adjustment terms, the process would succeed only if short-run trade relief actually promoted long-run adaptation. This is unlikely unless the plan includes steps painful to the parties that develop it: plant closings that cost jobs, wage restraint, burdensome investment commitments, and so forth. It would be hard for competing firms and their unions to reach agreement on taking these steps. So there would be a very strong temptation to base planning on the most optimistic assumptions, thereby postponing adjustment measures. The trade relief component of the package could reinforce this false optimism by creating an immediate economic environment in which prices could be raised and wages kept high.

The question then becomes who would insist on a "realistic, hardheaded" approach, to borrow the words of the Democrats? Who would supply the pressure to replace the forces of international competition? Firm leaders, whose previous *incapacity* to adapt had gotten them into a pickle? Labor leaders? Representatives of the very government agencies—Commerce, Labor, Agriculture—most likely to embrace the producer perspective?

Under the Heinz bill, the USITC could, in theory, act as the ultimate enforcer, rejecting the plan if it proved inadequate, and thus release the President from the pressure to implement the remedy. Specific funds might be allocated for adjustment activities like retooling, retraining, and job counseling, perhaps drawn from tariff revenues generated by temporary protection. This would involve the broad community of officials and institutions whose day-to-day business is unemployment assistance and vocational training: for them, worker mobility would be a sign of success, not failure.

Yet, if trade-specific adjustment activity were to grow very substantial in size—and it would need to grow large in order to play a role commensurate with the scope of the problem—it could develop the same sort of political vulnerabilities which beset TAA. The retraining community, as one example,

---

10. For more details, see *Congressional Record*, 20 November 1985.

might grow querulous when resources for trade-displaced labor exceeded resources for workers made jobless by other causes. One can hear critics asking why firms and workers that had already gotten trade protection should also get categorical money for *their* special adjustment needs. Further, an adjustment budget in the billions would likely become a political target at a time when other domestic spending remains under tight constraint.

These are some of the political problems that broad, trade-specific adjustment approaches would need to overcome. If they are not overcome, *adjustment-cum-protection* is likely to be no more, for the 1980s and 1990s, than *adjustment-as-alternative-to-protection* was for the 1960s and 1970s: a policy idea useful at the margin as a weapon in the political arsenal for liberal trade, but difficult to apply across the board.

Other Targeted Approaches to Displaced Workers

Since 1981, several state and local efforts have been mounted, often with national funding, to assist displaced workers. These programs include: the Job Training Partnership Act; several demonstration projects; and the Downriver Program. These programs have stated objectives that are similar to those enunciated by TAA, namely shortening the duration of unemployment and minimizing earnings losses. However, the new programs focus almost exclusively on employment-related services and retraining and provide practically no income maintenance.

JOB TRAINING PARTNERSHIP ACT

Title III of the Job Training Partnership Act of 1982 contains provisions for aiding displaced workers. A worker is eligible if he is permanently displaced and has little opportunity of returning to his previous industry or occupation. This eligibility test deemphasizes the location of declining industries and instead emphasizes the characteristics of individual workers.

The act provides a fixed, formula-based level of federal support for state-directed efforts to assist displaced workers through programs for retraining, job search, relocation, placement, and job development and support services. Income support is not available. The total federal budget for Title III is about $200 million annually. Combined with nonfederal matching funds, Title III is supposed to serve the needs of about 100,000 displaced workers annually.

A preliminary analysis of Title III indicates that some 47 percent of Title III projects provide on-the-job training, 45 percent provide classroom training, and 43 percent give job-search services. The preliminary analysis suggests that relocation assistance is little used.

DISLOCATED WORKER DEMONSTRATION PROGRAM

Six sites that experienced dislocation were selected by the Department of Labor in 1982 and asked to design and operate adjustment programs during fiscal year 1983. The programs were supposed to offer a full range of employment services, including on-the-job and classroom training, and relocation assistance.[11]

The highest placement rates were found among workers taking on-the-job training, while lower rates were found among those taking classroom training. Regardless of the type of assistance provided, reemployed workers experienced a wage loss that was greater the longer the worker had remained unemployed.

DOWNRIVER PROGRAM

The Downriver Community Conference Economic Readjustment Activity Program (DCCERA) refers to a program of assistance to workers displaced from five automobile and automobile-related plants in Southwestern Wayne County, Michigan. All of the plants closed permanently during the summer of 1980 and all workers were eligible to participate in an assistance program. The types of assistance made available included the full array of employment services and on-the-job and classroom training. Following substantial "outreach" efforts, 50 percent of the workers eligible to participate in the program actually enrolled.

Based on a sample of 1,000 workers, half of whom participated in the program and half of whom were similarly unemployed but ineligible for participation, the program increased the probability of reemployment from under 60 percent to over 72 percent. Program effects were largest for blacks and for less-skilled and less-educated workers.

---

11. The six sites were Alameda County, California; Buffalo, New York; Lehigh Valley, Pennsylvania; Milwaukee, Wisconsin; the Mid-Willamette Valley, Oregon; and Yakima County, Washington.

Displaced workers received lower wages on their post-layoff job. Program participants in the Downriver Project, however, had significantly smaller losses than nonparticipants: weekly earnings of these workers were roughly 25 percent above what they would have been in the absence of the program.

Lessons From Targeted Job Programs

The evidence from small-scale demonstration projects suggests that properly packaged employment services can reduce the duration of unemployment. Program participation can also reduce earnings losses. Retraining is often helpful. Many displaced workers, however, do not require nor are they interested in retraining. For these experienced workers, job counseling and job seeking services may be sufficient. But employment services without income support will probably never become a popular alternative to trade protection.

4 Past Alternatives to Long-Term Protection

In addition to Trade Adjustment Assistance (TAA), the United States has tried certain other alternatives to long-term special protection. The main alternative is the escape clause embodied in section 201 of the Trade Act of 1974 and Article XIX of the GATT. The escape clause never came to play a central role, because it was discretionary, because it was time-limited, because it implicitly favored tariffs rather than quotas, because it did not envisage selective restrictions, and because more attractive political avenues were open to troubled industries. However, some of the best industry adjustment stories in US experience have resulted from escape clause protection.

Two additional measures, antitrust policy and tax policy, are gaining attention as ingredients in the government's recipe to help industries adjust to international competition.

Escape Clause Relief

How does escape clause relief compare with other forms of special protection?[1] To answer this question, a sample of 16 manufacturing industries (table 4.1) was examined, representing nearly all industries that secured escape clause relief during the years 1950 to 1983.[2] In each of these cases the US International Trade Commission (USITC) made an affirmative finding that imports were a major source of injury, and the President responded by implementing some form of trade protection.

---

1. This section is adapted from Lawrence and DeMasi (1986).

2. This sample includes all escape clause cases in manufacturing during the years 1970–83, except the earthenware industry (excluded because of lack of readily available information) (USITC 1982).

45

TABLE 4.1   **Sample of manufacturing industries that received escape clause protection**

Industry	Years of protection	Trade coverage[a] (million dollars)	Type of protection
Watches	1954–67	55	tariff
Bicycles	1955–68	25	tariff
Clothespins	1957–62	1	tariff
	1979–82	2	quota
Stainless steel flatware	1958–67	9	tariff-rate quota
	1971–76	4	tariff-rate quota
Carpets	1962–73	30	tariff
Sheet glass	1962–74	30	tariff
Pianos	1970–74	9	tariff
Ball bearings	1974–78	60	tariff
Specialty steel	1976–80	213	quota
	1983–87	313	tariff-rate quota
Televisions	1977–82	412[b]	OMA
Nonrubber footwear	1977–81	1,179[b]	OMA
High carbon ferrochromium	1978–82	99	tariff
CB radios	1978–81	61	tariff
Bolts, nuts, and large screws	1979–82	375	tariff
Porcelain on steel cookware	1980–84	12	tariff
Motorcycles	1983–88	229	tariff-rate quota

a. Dollar value of imports in the beginning year of trade protection or a nearby year.
b. These figures refer to all imports, not just imports from the exporting countries restrained by orderly marketing agreements.

A review of these cases suggests that protection granted under the escape clause may at times be lengthy but it is in fact temporary. Of the 16 industries in the escape clause sample, only two continue to receive protection today (motorcycles and specialty steel). The standard duration of escape clause relief is about four years.

Of the 16 industries in the sample, 10 industries secured tariff increases, 2 industries were given orderly marketing arrangements (OMAs) that limit imports from principal suppliers, and 4 industries secured quota protection (including tariff-rate quotas).

The real test of industry adjustment comes with the removal of protection. Successful adjustment on the part of an industry implies that it can operate profitably without further government assistance or protection.[3] If the industry is no longer damaged by foreign trade—in the sense that labor and capital in the industry can once again earn normal returns—the industry has adjusted.

Based on this sample of trade-injured industries, successful adjustment can take one of two forms. Either an industry regains its competitive capacity by expanding, or it does so by contracting to a competitive core. In the former case, the industry may expand production, employment, and market share. In the latter case, surviving firms in the industry may focus production on a narrow product line and thereby secure a market niche. The most extreme form of contraction is industry exit, which happens when no strategy exists to compete against the overwhelming cost advantage of foreign producers.

In our sample of 16 industries, only 1 has adjusted through expansion (bicycles); 11 have adjusted through contraction; and, in the remaining four cases, it is too early to make an appraisal. Successful adjustment—in the sense that protection is no longer part of the picture—has occurred in the following industries: watches; bicycles; stainless steel flatwear; sheet glass; pianos; carpets; ball bearings; televisions; nonrubber footwear; high carbon ferrochromium; CB radios; and bolts, nuts, and screws.

The notion that they have adjusted successfully would probably come as a surprise to most participants in these industries. Indeed, at some point after their escape clause relief was suspended, 8 of the 12 industries petitioned the USITC for further relief—generally from unfair trade practices. However, the USITC usually denied further relief on the grounds that trade alone was not causing injury. These findings suggest that the industries in question (as well as those that did not bring new petitions) had adjusted to the point where they were no longer damaged by trade. This experience also indicates that the USITC can say "no," and that escape clause relief can thus be regarded as a temporary measure.

Five case examples illustrate the "successful" outcome of escape clause proceedings—one characterized by expansion and four characterized by contraction.

ADJUSTMENT WITH EXPANSION: BICYCLES

Among the successful adjusters, only the bicycle industry has expanded both employment and production to improve its performance in international trade.[4]

---

3. For adjustment to succeed all around, displaced workers must be satisfactorily employed elsewhere in the economy.

4. This section draws heavily on USITC (1982).

By changing the nature of its product, modernizing its plants, and taking advantage of extremely favorable demand conditions, US bicycle manufacturers reduced the share of imports in total US consumption from 28.1 percent in 1958 to 20.0 percent when protection expired in 1968.

In 1955, the US Tariff Commission determined that imported bicycles were seriously injuring the domestic industry. President Dwight D. Eisenhower partially suspended a 1947 tariff concession on the injured items, thereby raising the tariff level. This protection remained in effect until 1968. The success of the industry both during and after the removal of significant tariff protection was considerable.[5]

The general environment since 1955 has been extremely favorable for bicycle demand. The explosion of demand from youthful baby-boom cohorts in the 1950s and 1960s was followed by a rise in demand from adults eager to keep fit, explore the environment, and save on gasoline costs. Production increased from about 1.8 million bicycles in 1955 to 10.2 million bicycles in 1974. Producers were highly innovative; in the mid-1950s, they successfully introduced new middle-weight models that warded off the challenge from imported lightweights. New equipment was installed in newly constructed facilities located in lower cost areas. An increase in domestic demand in the 1970s caught the industry with insufficient capacity, and imports surged to 37.0 percent of the market in 1974. But the industry was able to restore its dominant position and, by 1979, the import share had been cut to 17.2 percent.

Recently, the bicycle industry has again experienced increasing competition from abroad. Import shares increased from 17.2 percent in 1979 to 30 percent in 1983. But the bicycle industry continued to demonstrate flexibility. Firms producing old style bicycles were supplanted by firms producing new styles; and modern operations replaced inefficient plants.

The overall performance of the bicycle industry seems to stand for the proposition that trade injury at one time does not preclude future success in the international marketplace. However, adjustment in the bicycle industry also highlights the conflict between modernizing facilities and preserving jobs. Each of the three largest bicycle manufacturers closed its plant and moved in the 1950s. The Huffy corporation left its small plant in Dayton,

---

5. In the Kennedy Round, concessions were made to reduce tariff protection beginning in 1968. In 1972, the current tariff rates of 5.5 percent ad valorem for lightweights and 11 percent for other categories were established.

Ohio, for new quarters in Celina, Ohio. In 1956, the American Machine and Foundry Company closed its midwest operations and built a new factory in Little Rock, Arkansas. And the second largest domestic company, Murray Ohio Manufacturing, moved its bicycle operation from Cleveland, Ohio, to Lawrenceburg, Tennessee.

Thus, in spite of the overall growth of the bicycle industry, most of the workers in the industry at the time of protection saw their jobs move elsewhere. Of the four unionized companies, workers from two lost their jobs with plant closures in 1956, and workers in the remaining two were laid off when their plants closed in the 1970s.

ADJUSTMENT WITH CONTRACTION AND NEW OWNERSHIP: TELEVISIONS

During the 1970s, the US color TV industry lost its competitiveness to Far Eastern producers, but not purely for labor cost reasons. Rather, the troubles of the domestic industry were caused by its own strategic miscalculations. Japan succeeded in the US market by aggressively innovating and foreseeing the untapped American demand for small TVs. The Japanese were the first to introduce integrated circuits and Sony's Trinitron system, which has fewer parts and improved picture quality. Before long, small TVs became associated with Japanese names and a market niche was established. With the failure of American companies to acknowledge the small TV market, they also failed to rapidly adopt the new technology.

When competitive problems arose for the TV industry, it sought protection via the USITC. In March 1977, the USITC unanimously determined that color TVs and subassemblies were being imported into the United States at a rate that caused serious injury. In response to this finding, President Jimmy Carter ordered the US Special Trade Representative (STR) to negotiate a three-year orderly marketing arrangement (OMA) with Japan. The OMA was soon undercut by surging imports from Taiwan and Korea. As a result, in February 1979, the STR concluded OMAs with these countries as well. Before the OMAs expired in 1980, the USITC conducted another investigation and determined that the Japanese OMA should expire as planned in 1980, but the OMAs with Korea and Taiwan should be extended. President Carter agreed, and the Korea and Taiwan OMAs expired in 1982.

The OMAs were of little help to the US industry (Baranson 1981, pp. 110–12). By the time the massive flow of imports was arrested with the

Taiwan and Korea agreement, four years had passed since the industry had voiced its need for import relief. Further, the OMAs may have partially contributed to basic changes in the structure of American industry. The Japanese, prevented by the OMA from securing a greater share in the US market, established more production facilities in the United States. In 1972, of the 17 firms producing televisions, 2 were Japanese-owned; by 1983, of the 17 firms in the industry, 12 firms were foreign-owned, and 8 of those were Japanese-owned.

Production by the color TV industry has increased steadily since the 1970s. Employment, however, declined considerably. Of the 32 percent decline in employment that occurred during the period from 1977 to 1983, 27.5 percentage points are probably attributable to the growth in foreign sourcing. Improvements in productivity accounted for the remaining 4.5 percentage points (USITC 1984a).

As a percentage of net sales, US R&D spending in the color TV industry declined from 4.2 percent in 1976 to 2.4 percent in 1982. Thus, the United States has become more dependent on foreign innovations. Indeed, Japanese firms have used their profits from the US market and elsewhere to develop new products such as video-recorders. The presence of Japanese firms ensures more rapid adoption of new technologies in the United States, but it also reflects an erosion in American technological leadership in this industry.

The objective of the OMA was to prevent injury to domestic firms and workers. From the perspective of firms, protection yielded higher profits. But protection also induced the major Far Eastern competitors to locate in the United States, thereby transforming foreign competition into domestic competition. In the end, the transformed industry was once again able to meet competition from abroad without continued protection. From the perspective of labor, however, the transition dislocated many workers and permanently reduced the number of job opportunities.

ADJUSTMENT WITH CONTRACTION: NONRUBBER FOOTWEAR

The nonrubber footwear industry's adjustment involved substantial transformation and entailed both contraction and modernization. With and without the aid of protection, the industry has undergone substantial transformation. During World War II, US producers supplied 100 percent of the domestic market. In 1983, they supplied only 36 percent of the market. Data for production, imports, and apparent consumption of nonrubber footwear provide stark evidence of how the US industry has contracted and foreign imports have expanded. During the period 1960 to 1983, US production decreased by 43 percent; imports grew by 2,087 percent; and apparent consumption increased by 47 percent (USITC 1984c).

The dominance of imports in the American market came in two major surges. The first was in the early 1960s with increased imports from Italy and Japan; the second was during the late 1960s and early 1970s with increased imports from Korea and Taiwan. The reasons for foreign success in capturing the US market stem mainly from lower foreign labor costs. Footwear is a labor-intensive industry and wages in the Far East are about 25 percent of US wages. In addition, the Europeans have maintained an advantage in the "upscale" section of the industry through styling and fashion.

How has the US industry adjusted to international competition? In 1977, after a long and hard battle involving many industry petitions filed with the USITC, the STR finally negotiated a three-year OMA with Taiwan and Korea, and Trade Adjustment Assistance was guaranteed for the nonrubber footwear industry. In 1980, the USITC began another investigation to determine whether relief should extend beyond the OMA expiration date of 1981. The Commission unanimously decided that the industry could stand on its own.[6] As imports continued to increase their market share, successful firms have sought to compensate for high domestic labor costs and to pursue targeted marketing strategies. To improve productivity and defray the high labor cost, the US industry installed cost-effective and technologically advanced equipment. To a limited extent, the industry sought lower labor costs by establishing offshore production facilities in countries such as Canada, Mexico, Haiti, India, and England, and by importing footwear for sale through established distribution networks in the US market. Within the United States, firms have found lower labor costs in the South and in the West.

Equally important is concentration in submarkets where competition is less intense. Generally, the US industry has made headway in the middle-priced

6. The nonrubber footwear industry remains profitable despite five post-OMA requests for USITC investigations for unfair trade practices or escape clause action. These USITC investigations have all resulted in negative decisions either by the USITC or, as in the most recent case, by the President.

and high-priced submarkets. Recent success in these segments of the market is illustrated by the 5 percent decline in the volume of imports of high-priced footwear from Brazil, Italy, France, and Spain over the period 1979 to 1984. Correspondingly, the US industry has moved out of submarkets that have come under particularly strong import competition—for example, inexpensive women's sandals.

The industry's transition meant fewer firms and falling employment. The number of firms in the United States dropped from 597 in 1969 to 248 in 1982. Many of the surviving firms became manufacturer-importers. Employment also fell dramatically, from 242,600 in 1960 to 120,000 in 1984.

The pace of adjustment was too rapid for congressional tastes. In section 249 of the Trade and Tariff Act of 1984, the Congress, at the insistence of Senator John C. Danforth (R-Mo.), altered the escape clause to require that prior plant closings be taken into account as evidence of present injury, even if the surviving firms are healthy, and that profits earned from captive imports should not be considered in determining the industry's profitability. Section 249 was a pointed congressional criticism of the 1984 USITC finding that the footwear industry was not injured by imports. A new case was brought; in May 1985, the USITC voted unanimously that the industry was entitled to escape clause relief; and, in a novel departure, the USITC recommended a system of quota auctions (rather than assigned quotas) that would reduce imports by 100 million pairs (USITC 1985). President Ronald Reagan, however, decided to deny trade relief of any kind. The plight of the footwear industry was taken up by the supporters of legislation to tighten textile quotas. The legislation passed both houses of Congress but was vetoed by President Reagan on December 17, 1985.

ADJUSTMENT WITH CONTRACTION: STAINLESS STEEL TABLE FLATWEAR

In several cases, protection slowed the movement of resources out of the affected industries and presumably reduced dislocation by spreading adjustment over a longer period.[7] In these cases, temporary protection can be judged successful. However, in a few cases resources were actually attracted to the sector and were later forced to leave.

---

7. This section draws heavily on USITC (1982).

Stainless steel table flatware is just such an example. In 1959, President Eisenhower partially suspended tariff concessions on several stainless steel items and imposed a tariff-rate quota. In addition, between 1958 and 1966, the Japanese government imposed a voluntary export quota. As a consequence of quota and tariff protection, employment grew from 3,057 in 1958 to 3,763 in 1967. In 1967, although the US Tariff Commission voted to extend protection, President Lyndon B. Johnson took no action. The industry was later granted an additional five years of protection from 1971 to 1976 as a result of negotiations with Japan. However, in this later period, imports captured a growing share of US consumption. Despite a tariff-rate quota in effect between 1971 and 1976, and increasing US consumption of flatware between 1969 and 1980, employment declined to 2,284 in 1977 and the number of firms fell from 15 to 7. The industry was later reduced to the point where only the largest company, Oneida, was able to compete successfully by modernizing and successful marketing. Adjustment ultimately prevailed but only indirectly: protection in the early period attracted resources, only to be expelled later.

ADJUSTMENT WITH INDUSTRY EXIT: HIGH CARBON FERROCHROMIUM

Cost competition in high carbon ferrochromium (HCF) has driven US firms to virtual extinction.[8] From 1978 to 1982, trade protection temporarily slowed the pace of an inevitable decline, but the industry's inability to secure a market niche or substantially reduce the cost of production left little chance for survival.

The United States has few available reserves of chromite. However, for many years, higher productivity enabled the United States to offset the cost disadvantage of importing the essential raw material from South Africa. During the 1960s, South Africa began to develop and expand the necessary technology to process ore and produce HCF. Today, South Africa is the world's leading producer of HCF. The success of the South African industry stems from an inexpensive source of power (coal), ample reserves of chromite, and a low cost of labor. Also, HCF production sites are located close to ore

---

8. High carbon ferrochromium, produced by processing chromite, is used as a source of chromium in stainless steel. Chromite reserves are concentrated in southern Africa, which accounts for 97 percent of world reserves.

mines, thereby minimizing transportation cost in the production process (USITC 1981). For the United States, improved technology in the South African industry meant greater competitive pressure.

This change in world market dominance is reflected in US imports of chromite and HCF. In 1971, of US imports of chromium-related products, 87 percent was chromite, and 12 percent was ferrochromium. However, by 1981, the composition had changed considerably: 50 percent was chromite, and 50 percent was ferrochromium (US Department of Interior 1983, p. 4).

In response to growing international competition, the US industry petitioned the USITC on numerous occasions and finally received a three-year tariff increase in 1978. In 1981, before protection was to expire, the Commission recommended an additional year of protection, which the President granted.

During the period of protection, and indeed even to the present, the industry has followed an adjustment path that pointed to extinction. The inability of the HCF industry to endure severe competition stems from the characteristics of the product itself. HCF is used heavily in the production of stainless steel, an industry that is highly conscious of its input prices. There is no product differentiation for comparable grades of HCF, and therefore, no scope to find a secure market niche. Success in the HCF market depends solely on price. A fundamental shift occurred in the world market of HCF, and US technology could no longer compensate for the costs and inefficiencies associated with transporting raw materials.

In 1977, just before protection was granted, five firms produced HCF in the United States. In 1982 when protection expired, only two firms operated. Over the 1970s, imports as a proportion of US production increased from 39 percent in 1972 to 148 percent in 1980. Profits were volatile over the 1970s: from 1974 to 1978, profits plummeted; they recovered slightly in 1978–1979, and began another descent in 1980. In 1984, only one firm remained in operation (MacAlloy), even though two others have retained their HCF related equipment but produce other ferroalloy products. The survival of MacAlloy depends on the 1982 presidential decision to upgrade the National Defense Stockpile of chromium over a 10-year period.

LESSONS FROM THE ESCAPE CLAUSE

Trade protection may provide a respite for industries to modernize, but modernization is not always the answer. First, the problems confronting industries such as those which produce sheet glass or Wilton and velvet carpets stemmed primarily from competition from cost-effective domestically available substitutes. Exit rather than modernization was the appropriate strategy. Similarly, for industries making undifferentiated products in which costs alone determine sales, modernization may not be able to restore lost competitiveness, as illustrated by HCF and CB radios. Even when modernization is feasible, it may require a change in ownership (as with color TVs), a change in plant location (as with bicycles), or significant contraction and a narrowing of market focus (as with nonrubber footwear).

In the escape clause cases, protection was usually temporary, and thus firms had every incentive to take advantage of the respite to adjust. The USITC has shown remarkable resistance to political and industry pressure (witness its negative decisions on automobiles in 1980 and footwear in 1984). The contrast between the relatively successful adjustment of industries that obtained protection via the USITC route and the lack of adjustment in industries that obtained protection via political routes (such as textiles and dairy products) carries an important lesson.

International Supervision of Safeguards

The term "safeguards" refers to national mechanisms for responding to imports that "harm" the importing country's competing industries.[9] These mechanisms often take the form of increased tariffs, quantitative restrictions, or "voluntary" restraints by the exporting countries.

The recent legal history of safeguards begins with the US escape clause. The US–Mexico Reciprocal Trade Agreement of 1943 contained one of the earliest versions of the escape clause. This clause was a popular feature with Congress and, in 1947, as the United States and 21 other countries began negotiating the text of an International Trade Organization (ITO) and the General Agreement on Tariffs and Trade (GATT), President Harry S Truman issued an Executive Order requiring that an escape clause be included in every trade agreement entered into under the authority of the US Reciprocal Trade Agreements program. Thus, the GATT escape clause (Article XIX) was a direct lineal descendant of the US–Mexico Trade Agreement provision.

Article XIX of GATT furnishes the principal international norm relating to "safeguards." It allows temporary imposition of import restraints when

9. This section is adapted from Jackson (1986).

increasing imports have caused (or threatened) serious injury to a competing domestic industry. Unfortunately, major ambiguities in the Article XIX language, including questions such as the definition of "increasing imports," or "cause of injury," or "industry," render Article XIX relatively impotent to bring national safeguards measures under international discipline. In addition, the permitted responses to safeguard actions, often termed "compensation" and "retaliation," have become increasingly unusable. Not only does the GATT machinery work in a ponderous fashion, but exporting countries affected by safeguards are also often reluctant to worsen their trading relations with importing countries by demanding "compensation" or imposing "retaliation."

Although Article XIX is the central and most prominent safeguard provision of GATT, a number of other measures taken under GATT (or in evasion of GATT) can also be termed safeguards. For example, GATT Article XXVIII provides a means by which a contracting party can permanently withdraw a tariff "binding," namely an obligation as to a maximum tariff. GATT Articles XII and XVIII provide exceptions for balance of payments difficulties. These measures, as well as other provisions of Article XVIII designed for developing countries, often provide a GATT-legal cover for border import restraints that are motivated by safeguards policies. Finally, there are various techniques other than those permitted by GATT. The most prominent in recent years has been the "voluntary" export restraint.

THE MOST-FAVORED-NATION RULE

A controversial issue concerning the application of Article XIX has been the question whether a remedy must be applied in a nondiscriminatory manner, that is, on a most-favored-nation (MFN) basis (Bronckers 1985). The MFN clause of GATT Article I requires each GATT member to accord all other GATT members the most favorable trade concessions that it grants to any foreign country. What does this mean in the context of a safeguard action?

If a country invokes Article XIX then it might apply either tariffs or quantitative restraints. If it utilized tariffs, there would be one tariff rate for the products of all GATT nations and the MFN requirement would be satisfied. If it utilized quantitative restrictions, the MFN concept becomes more difficult. Usually quotas are granted on a country-by-country basis. Country quotas are inherently discriminatory in the sense that they seldom reach the same result that the operation of the price mechanism would achieve. Nevertheless, under GATT practice, it is generally considered that the MFN requirement has been satisfied if country quotas are established on the basis of the amount or proportion of trade that each country supplied during a recent historical period. This procedure discriminates against new entrants to the market—a source of considerable bitterness for developing countries.

A government might expressly desire to depart from the MFN application of Article XIX. Often the argument is made that it is wise to do so, because only a few countries have "caused" the increased imports that provoke the use of Article XIX. The "offending" countries are those with rapid and recent gains in the importing country's market. By way of justification for a discriminatory approach, it is sometimes asked: "Why should countries that are not responsible for the increase in imports bear the burden of an escape clause action?"

The policy counterargument is that recent entrants to the market are doing exactly what they are supposed to do under the world trade system inaugurated by the GATT. They are producing better and less expensive goods and the market is buying their products. To penalize those countries is to punish the very nations that are playing by the rules of a liberal trade system.

Those are the basic policy arguments. Now let us turn to the legal arguments. The language of Article XIX states that the injured contracting party shall be free "to suspend the obligation" of GATT which is deemed to be linked to the increased imports. The language is not explicit as to which obligations may be suspended. It is argued that the MFN obligations of GATT Article I fall within the scope of obligations that can be suspended. For this reason, it is argued, Article XIX legally and technically allows discriminatory import restraints.

A counterargument, focusing on the language of the GATT, is that the MFN obligation of Article I can in no way be deemed responsible for the increased imports. The increased imports are related causally only to domestic demand for imports of the goods *generally*, not to imports from any particular source. It is a matter of indifference to domestic consumers from where the goods come. An important interpretive practice in GATT is invoked in this analysis. The 1948 negotiations for the International Trade Organization produced an interpretive note inserted in the draft Havana charter that called for the nondiscriminatory application of safeguard measures. In 1953, a GATT Working Party indicated that the same view was taken for GATT

Article XIX. This has been the basis of the legal argument that the GATT escape clause requires MFN application.

Starting in the Tokyo Round safeguards negotiations, the European Community made policy and legal arguments for discriminatory measures under Article XIX. This position aroused intense opposition from the many developing countries that see themselves as natural targets of discrimination.

The United States position in the GATT negotiations has varied a bit. Early in the Tokyo Round, the United States strongly supported a nondiscriminatory approach. At one point, the United States seemed to relax this stance. In recent years, however, the United States has again taken a strong pro-MFN approach to Article XIX.

Where does all this leave us? As is true of so many legal issues in the GATT (or other international agreements), it is hard to say with complete assurance what the interpretation of an international obligation should be. It does seem likely that, if the matter were to go to a GATT panel, the panel would rule—on the basis of the interpretive note to the Havana Charter and the 1953 GATT Working Party report—that MFN is required for Article XIX remedies.

EXPORT RESTRAINTS

One of the most frequent safeguard actions in recent decades has been the export restraint, imposed by an exporting country at the request of an importing country. Industry-to-industry restraints are sometimes arranged directly between firms in the exporting country and firms in the importing country. A variety of terms have been used for these restraints, including orderly marketing agreement (OMA), voluntary export restraints (VER), voluntary restraint agreement (or arrangement, VRA), and interindustry arrangements.

These arrangements are most troublesome. One problem is their "lack of transparency"—many of the arrangements are secret. A related problem is that they are seldom subjected to the scrutiny of domestic or international proceedings. The arrangements often seem to result from barely concealed political favors rendered to domestic pressure groups. Finally, in most cases, the arrangements have dubious international legal status. They appear to violate the requirements of GATT Article XI (regarding export restraints) and they find no sanction in GATT Article XIX.

But the difficulty with GATT surveillance is quite pragmatic—who will make a formal complaint? The country that establishes the export restraint would hardly complain against itself in GATT. The importing country that signalled the need for restraint would hardly complain either, since the action is precisely what was hoped for. Other countries in GATT would find it difficult to complain, because they normally would not be able to establish harm to their own trade. Thus, there have been few formal cases in GATT concerning the use of export restraints as a safeguards measure.

For example, a possible complainant country in the GATT context, country C, feels that, as a result of an export restraint arrangement between A and B, exports of A have been diverted from the B market, thus putting greater competitive pressure on the market in C. This was basically the complaint of the US steel industry in a domestic proceeding brought in 1976. However, the US government declined to bring a case in GATT on behalf of the US industry because adequate evidence of actual diversion or harm was not established. A similar case, involving Japanese and Korean steel, occurred in 1984–85.

A NEW SAFEGUARDS CODE

One objective of the Tokyo Round of negotiations, as reflected in the September 1973 Tokyo Ministerial Declaration, was the development of a new Safeguards Code. The new code was supposed to enhance international discipline on the use of safeguards. This objective of the Tokyo Round largely ended in failure. The contracting parties could not come to a mutual agreement, despite extensive sessions and hard work. The Director General's report at the end of the Tokyo Round spelled out the difficulties and listed a number of issues that had been taken up in the negotiations, including:

- discriminatory or non-discriminatory application of safeguards measures

- degressivity of safeguards measures

- time limits

- requirement of adjustment assistance

- sharing the burden among importing nations of disruptive or injurious imports coming from one or a few exporting nations

- market disruption and serious injury definitions

- provisions for international surveillance.

The negotiating parties did agree that a committee of the GATT contracting parties should continue negotiations, and that committee still meets today. At the November 1982 Ministerial Meeting, the Ministerial Declaration called for a safeguards understanding to be drawn up by the Council for adoption by the contracting parties not later than their 1983 session. This deadline was not achieved. Observers who are optimistic suggest that progress continues; others, of course, are entitled to remain skeptical.

Meanwhile, very little exists in the way of legal norms with respect to economic adjustment. Some sort of obligation might be implied from the more general clauses of GATT. For example, Article XXXVI of GATT expresses a desire that developed countries provide favorable and acceptable conditions for access to world markets for the products of developing countries. Likewise, in Article XXXVII of GATT, developed countries are called upon to "give active consideration to the adoption of other measures designed to provide greater scope for the development of imports from Less-Developed Contracting Parties. . . ." Article XXXVIII of GATT reinforces this viewpoint, with general admonitions for contracting parties to collaborate "in seeking feasible methods to expand trade for the purpose of economic development." These general admonitions have not so far been translated into practice.

It is apparent that the international rules centered in GATT concerning safeguards and adjustment are too weak and ambiguous to provide an effective level of discipline on national measures. Attempts to reform the safeguards or adjustment process in the international trade institutions have not so far yielded much progress. If greater international discipline on national safeguard measures is feasible, how might a new arrangement be shaped? Four suggestions may be offered.

First, a "two-tier" approach has been suggested from time to time, and has much appeal. The basic concept is that those governments who so desire would enter into a mutual agreement by which certain privileges—such as the right to avoid the payment of "compensation"—would be accorded by the other code signatories in circumstances where rigorous escape clause criteria were fulfilled. The agreement would remain open for future accession by all nonparticipants. The prerequisites for a safeguard measure—namely increasing imports and related serious injury—would be defined more precisely. Likewise, the range of permissible remedies, such as the time period for degressivity, and the nature of the remedy (quantitative restriction or tariff), could be better specified.

Second, an agreement might begin with an extensive set of obligations for "transparency." These obligations could well entail full reporting of all safeguard measures and the amount of trade affected. The reporting obligation should fall on both the importing country and the exporting country. Thus, countries who seem to be abusing safeguard measures might be noticed more rapidly.

Third, a requirement of adjustment assistance might be considered a prerequisite for the privileges of the agreement. Governments might appropriately be asked to offer a program for downsizing the domestic industry, including retraining and early retirement benefits.

Fourth and finally, careful thought must be given to the necessary international institutions to make such a system operate effectively. At a minimum, this would require a Safeguards Committee, charged with receiving reports, meeting periodically, questioning national practices, and bringing cases when appropriate.

Other Policies For Troubled Industries

In this section, we survey the use of antitrust policy and tax policy to further adjustment by US industries facing foreign competition. These auxiliary measures have gained greater attention in the 1980s.

ANTITRUST POLICY

Adjustment to import competition often involves consolidation through mergers and other arrangements.[10,11] For example, since 1977, faced with

---

10. This section is adapted from Kwoka (1986).

11. Consolidation in the face of import competition is a common experience among industrial countries. For example, a close look at trade-impacted German firms shows an overwhelming presence of adjustment through consolidation. Merger activities were significantly above average in the German iron and steel industry (between 1967 and 1971 more than one-third of the existing firms merged), in nonferrous metals production, in aircraft and aerospace industry (between 1967 and 1971 the share of merging firms was similar to that of the iron and steel industry), in the cellulose paper and board industry, in textiles, and in food processing. Meanwhile, cartelization was relatively high in iron and steel, nonferrous metals, shipbuilding, leather products, fine ceramics, and textiles (Dicke and Glismann 1986).

slack demand at home and competition from abroad, the US auto and steel industries have embarked on a wave of mergers, joint ventures, and equity purchases. In autos, these include Renault's half-interest in AMC (1978); Chrysler's equity stake in Peugeot (1978); Ford's partial acquisition of Mazda (1979); GM's increased equity stake in Isuzu and new stake in Suzuki (1982); and GM's joint venture with Toyota (1984). Steel industry examples include the LTV-Youngstown merger (1977); Nisshin's equity stake in Wheeling-Pittsburgh (1984); joint ventures involving Kawasaki and Kaiser (1984), Nippon Kokan and National Steel (1984), and LTV and Sumitomo (1985); and the LTV-Republic Steel merger (1983). The recent experience of the auto and steel industries demonstrates three things about the antitrust dimensions of trade-induced consolidation.

First, most proposed consolidations have ultimately passed antitrust scrutiny. Some consolidations entailed close policy decisions, and were modified as a condition of approval. But US antitrust policy has seldom prevented the consolidation of firms in troubled industries.

Second, a pattern has arisen in which transnational associations raise fewer antitrust concerns than combinations involving two domestic producers. Import restraints serve to reduce direct competition between US and foreign producers. This adds to the antitrust burden of, for example, an LTV merger with Republic Steel, but simplifies Nippon Kokan's case for acquisition of National Steel. The numerous equity purchases plus one joint venture in the auto industry, as well as several joint ventures in steel, exemplify this phenomenon. While this is the logical consequence of import restraints, it was probably an unintended effect.

Third, some recent instances of consolidation have turned on quite elusive benefits. Often, structural changes have been argued to reduce costs in ways that seemingly could have been done anyway. Although the precise necessity for merger may not be clear, the antitrust agencies have shown considerable sympathy with the claims. In fact, sympathy has now become explicit policy. President Reagan recently accepted a unanimous recommendation by the Cabinet-level Economic Planning and Domestic Planning councils to seek a modification of antitrust laws so that trade-impacted industries are exempted from antitrust restrictions on mergers.[12]

---

12. *Washington Post,* 6 December 1985, A1; *Business Week,* 9 December 1985, p. 38; *Financial Times,* 24 December 1985, p. 2.

The new attitude of tolerance for corporate mergers raises the risk that firms in trade-impacted industries will propose unjustified mergers when less permanent arrangements would serve the same ends. As a plausible alternative to corporate mergers, the US International Trade Commission should be empowered to permit plant closing arrangements and negotiated side payments between firms.

TAX POLICY FOR CORPORATIONS

Corporations contemplating a plant closing are likely to have significant net operating loss carryforwards from past operations.[13] They might also have investment credit carryforwards. The magnitude of these carryforwards will depend on the circumstances. For example, steel producers that have embarked on costly programs of plant modernization may have significant net operating losses, in part because the industry is depressed and in part because of the rapid system of depreciation that applies to post–1981 investments (the Accelerated Cost Recovery System). By contrast, apparel manufacturers that use labor-intensive production methods may be able to shut down before accumulating large net operating losses.

The benefit of a tax loss is potential in the sense that a corporation must already have, or be able to generate, sufficient taxable income to absorb the loss. Thus, the tax consequences of closing a plant depend on whether a corporation (or its affiliates) have other ongoing operations that generate sufficient taxable income to absorb the loss, or, if not, what happens to the corporation after its plant is closed.

Although a corporation closing a plant may otherwise be in poor financial shape, carryforwards of net operating loss and investment tax credits can represent significant economic assets. If the corporation decides to enter a new industry, it can use net operating loss carryforwards to offset taxable income derived from its new operations. Once the net operating loss has been used up, carryforwards of investment tax credits will further reduce its tax liability. In sum, its carryforwards may give the firm a tax advantage over potential competitors.

Even when a corporation with tax carryforwards has a tax advantage over all other new entrants in a viable industry, the acquisition of an ongoing,

---

13. This section is adapted from Horst (1986).

tax-paying corporation will often result in more immediate and more profitable use of tax benefits than entering a new industry. If restrictions on "trafficking" in tax carryforwards are circumvented, merger or acquisition can result in the immediate utilization of tax carryforwards, whereas entry into new industries yields deferred and possibly uncertain benefits. All other things being equal, corporations with tax carryforwards are apt to prefer merger with, or acquisition of, another corporation to entry into new industries. In other words, tax policy, like antitrust policy, exhibits a bias in favor of mergers rather than less permanent consolidation arrangements.

As a matter of public policy, corporations that close plants should be encouraged to enter viable new industries, rather than to undertake mergers or acquisitions with existing tax-paying corporations. In the context of a larger adjustment package, with appropriate conditions attached, the US International Trade Commission could further this goal by acquiring the tax carryforwards resulting from net operating losses and investment credits, and then simply retire the carryforwards. The USITC would pay "face value" for the carryforwards, where face value is defined as the amount of the net operating loss carryforward times the marginal corporate tax rate (currently 46 percent), or the amount of the investment tax credit carryforward. Judging from experience with "safe harbor" leasing, the market value of tax carryforwards may be significantly less than their face value. If the USITC paid face value for the tax carryforwards, that would provide a significant incentive for corporations in declining industries to enter new industries rather than merge with existing firms.

TAX POLICY FOR UNEMPLOYED WORKERS

The main tax issues for unemployed workers relate to the taxability of benefits and the deductibility of expenses associated with changing employment. The primary benefits *received* by displaced employees and the taxability of those benefits are as follows:

• *Severance pay* is taxable.

• *Government-paid unemployment benefits* are not taxable unless the total of those benefits plus adjusted gross income for tax purposes exceeds $18,000 on a joint return and $12,000 on a single individual's tax return. If the total exceeds the threshold, 50 percent of benefits in excess of the threshold are taxable.

• *Supplemental employment benefits* are taxable.

• *Reimbursement for moving expenses* is taxable but, as noted below, qualified moving expenses are deductible.

• *Gain on the sale of a principal residence* is tax deferred if a new principal residence is purchased and used within two years (plus or minus) of the date on which the former residence was sold.

• *Reimbursement by an employer for a loss on the sale of a residence* is taxable.

The primary expenses *incurred* by displaced employees and the deductibility of those expenses are as follows:

• *Moving expenses* are deductible if: the new work place is at least 35 miles further from a taxpayer's former residence than his old work place was; and the individual or spouse is a full-time employee for 39 of the 52 weeks of the year following the date of his or her arrival in the general location of the new work place.

• *"Indirect" moving expenses* (e.g., travel expenses incident to the purchase of a new residence) are deductible up to a fixed dollar amount.

• *Job-necessitated travel and transportation expenses* are deductible.

• *Job search expenses* and *education and retraining expenses* are deductible if and only if related to an individual's current trade or business. Expenses of finding or training for a job in a new trade or business are not deductible.

From the perspective of a displaced employee, the last provision—which denies a deduction for job search and education expenses if those expenses relate to a *new* trade or business—seems indefensible. The "new trade or business" test should be dropped for displaced employees. At the same time, satisfactory criteria should be developed to identify displaced employees and to define job search and retraining costs that qualify for a deduction. As a start, the US International Trade Commission could certify workers who are displaced by import competition, and specify limits on qualified job search and retraining costs.

Lessons From Past Experience

While frequently instituted in the name of saving jobs, trade protection is rarely precise enough to assist the individual workers and communities affected by industrial decline. The strongest argument for trade protection is to allow a more orderly and humane contraction process than market forces might permit. However, the effects of protection are extremely costly when allowed to prevail over extended periods of time. Experience under the escape clause gives reason for cautious optimism on the question of time-limited, degressive protection.

The shift in national policies away from tariffs towards quotas under Article XIX has threatened the nondiscriminatory nature of the most-favored-nation principle. Export restraints have also become more prevalent. These restraints lack transparency and are rarely subject to domestic and international scrutiny. It is still not clear whether they can be considered legal under the current system since it is not in any one country's interest to initiate a formal case before the GATT.

Import restraints have served to reduce direct competition between US and foreign producers and thus make it easier for international joint ventures and equity purchases to take place. Current tax law tends to promote mergers and acquisitions because of large net operating and investment credit carryforwards, thus reducing the incentive to move into new industries. Personal tax law reflects this disincentive by limiting deductions for job search and education and retraining expenses. These expenses are currently only deductible when related to an individual's current trade or business.

Thus, in addition to placing more emphasis on the domestic escape clause, GATT Article XIX should be clarified and strengthened. Further, the ongoing negotiations should be accelerated in an effort to develop a new safeguards code that will more effectively ensure that national measures are directed towards adjustment. Tax and antitrust policies should also be used to provide relief and promote adjustment in trade-affected industries. All of these elements are contained in our proposal for a new adjustment strategy in chapter 5.

5 A New Trade Policy for Troubled Industries

The rationale for a new approach is simple: to provide a plausible alternative to new and embedded cases of special protection. We do not pretend that a new approach will convert organized labor and distressed industries into champions of free trade. But we do think that a new approach might persuade labor and management to cling somewhat less tenaciously to special protection as the only answer to the problems of troubled industries.

An old objection to trade adjustment assistance, voiced in the 1970s, is this: equivalent assistance should be provided to all dislocated workers and distressed firms—whether displaced by new product competition, geographic shifts in industrial advantage within the United States, or new competition from abroad.[1]

But this argument for equivalent assistance as between trade-impacted firms and workers, and other displaced firms and workers, ignores political reality. The Job Training Partnership Act (JTPA), for example, provides less than $3,000 of federal benefits per displaced worker, and no benefits to industry. The benefits of special protection can easily exceed $5,000 for every worker in the industry, not just displaced workers. The total annual transfer of resources from consumers to producers in just one instance of special protection, the automobile case, exceeded $2.6 billion annually. This figure dwarfs the magnitude of JTPA.

---

1. George P. Shultz, then Director of the Office of Management and Budget and subsequently Secretary of Treasury, was an early critic of special relief for trade-impacted workers in the context of the debate over the Trade Act of 1974. Other critics include Goldfarb (1980) and the American Enterprise Institute (1983). Frank (1977) favored an across-the-board assistance program but supported the continuation of TAA as an interim measure. A small start toward general assistance programs was made with the Comprehensive Employment Training Act of 1973 (CETA), and its successor, the Job Training Partnership Act of 1982 (JTPA). For a review of the present menu of across-the-board assistance, see CBO (1982), Orr (1986), and Podgursky (1984).

67

In practical budget terms it would not be possible to enlarge JTPA and other wide-angle programs to match the level of targeted benefits now provided by special protection. In January 1983, the total number of dislocated workers, defined as unemployed persons in a declining industry or a declining area, reached some 1.7 million persons. If benefits in the range of $10,000 per employee were extended to these dislocated workers and their firms, the budget cost would be huge, about $17 billion annually.[2]

A prospective budget expenditure of $17 billion would surely prompt ways to trim outlays per worker drastically. Beneficiaries of special protection will not, however, exchange their present menu of relief alternatives for a substantially leaner diet. The tension between budget realities and interest group realities means that, for the time being, a feasible alternative to special protection must remain targeted on trade-impacted industries.

A new objection to trade adjustment, voiced in the mid-1980s, is this: why should American industry and agriculture adjust to a dollar exchange rate that, at the end of 1985, remained overvalued, in trade competitiveness terms, by 25 percent or more?[3] This objection makes a great deal of sense when applied to the *overall* traded goods sector of the economy, a sector that produces about a quarter of US output. But within the traded goods sector, certain activities are protected far beyond the norm. The experience of Australia in the late 1970s and early 1980s (Gregory 1986), the United Kingdom in the 1970s (Cable 1986), Germany in the 1970s (Dicke and Glismann 1986), and the United States in the late 1970s suggests that specially protected industries still need to adjust, even after exchange rate overvaluation has disappeared. Based on this experience, we think there is little danger of too rapid or too extensive adjustment by US industries that now enjoy special protection.

Our plan for industries that receive, or might in the future seek, special protection has several elements, described in the body of this chapter. The

---

2. There would be some offset for a reduction in unemployment insurance (UI) now paid to dislocated workers. State unemployment benefits generally expire after 26 weeks and provide between $190 and $200 maximum a week. About 50 percent of unemployed workers meet the eligibility requirements for UI. As a high estimate, the unemployment benefits paid in 1983 to dislocated workers were about $4 billion (CBO 1982, pp. 26, 38).

3. Estimates of fundamental equilibrium exchange rates appear in Williamson (1985). After a substantial correction in most of 1985, the dollar remained overvalued, in trade competitiveness terms, by some 25 percent at the end of 1985 (Marris 1985).

basic thrust of the new approach can, however, be summarized in a few paragraphs.[4]

The plan calls for centralizing relief under a refurbished escape clause. Why the escape clause? This provision has been a durable, if underutilized, component of US trade policy for more than 40 years. It makes practical political sense to build on familiar foundations. Moreover, escape clause relief requires that injury be demonstrated in an adversarial setting, a useful means of weeding out unjustified claims. Finally, of all forms of special protection, escape clause relief has most reliably functioned in a time-limited fashion.

The purpose of relief under the new plan, as under the existing escape clause, is to provide temporary "breathing room" for orderly adjustment, not to provide a facade for indefinite protection. Publicly supported reinvestment is not part of the scheme; reinvestment decisions are left to private enterprise.

The US International Trade Commission is called upon to design a menu of relief alternatives, while the US Trade Representative (USTR) is charged with selecting the actual course to be followed. The relief provided should address both "domestic" causes of decline—unemployment from slow demand growth and fast productivity growth—and "international" causes of decline—unemployment from greater import penetration.

Assured funding for adjustment purposes is built into the plan. This is an important point: since general revenues are always scarce, self-financed options are a key ingredient of the relief menu. Self-financing is generated by tariffs, auctioned quotas, or taxes on the industry's products. In addition, this introduces the "user-cost" principle in funding adjustment.

The elimination of protection can serve a country's self-interest, regardless of what other countries might do. But as a matter of practical politics, major trading countries are unlikely to embrace a meaningful adjustment program without cooperative international efforts. Very little will be done to liberalize, for example, US sugar or apparel imports unless Europe and Japan agree to equally beneficial (and painful) adjustment measures. Thus, the plan calls for a new Safeguards and Adjustment Code that requires all signatories to undertake comparable obligations.[5]

---

4. The basic plan was spelled out in Hufbauer and Rosen (1983). Other commentators have likewise emphasized the importance of renewed attention on adjustment. See, for example, USTR (1984); Bailey (1984); Schultz and Schumacher (1984).

5. For a view of how a new Safeguards and Adjustment Code might fit into a new round of trade talks, see Hufbauer and Schott (1985).

The modalities of national programs may differ from country to country. The outline presented here is designed with the American political context in mind. Quite different approaches might work best in Japan or Germany. International agreement will, however, be required on certain common features: industries to be covered; time limits and benchmarks for adjustment; and the use of tariffs, auctioned quotas, and product taxes rather than quantitative restraints (QRs).

"Domestic" and "International" Causes of Decline

Problem industries face difficulty not only—and often not primarily—because foreign firms are gaining ground. Problem industries frequently face a combination of stagnant home demand and productivity gains that outstrip the meager growth of the home market. For example, steel companies throughout the world have suffered a decade of essentially zero growth.[6] In 1973–74, noncommunist world production averaged 543 million net tons of crude steel. At that time, many observers were predicting western world steel demand of 1,000 to 1,400 million tons by the mid-1980s. Instead, demand stagnated in response to two oil shocks and sustained world recession. In 1979, demand finally returned to its 1974 level, but since then steel shipments have fallen sharply. In 1982 and 1983, total western world steel production was approximately 100 million tons below its 1973–74 peak. The International Iron and Steel Institute recently predicted that, even by 1990, the noncommunist world would not reach its 1973–74 level of steel consumption. In short, we may well see 15 years of zero growth for the basic world industry. On top of stagnant demand, rising productivity has cut into employment.

Industries like the steel industry often confront shrinking employment even when they do not face rising imports. On top of these home-grown difficulties, imports may be capturing an ever-larger share of the domestic market.

These background conditions—common to steel, autos, meat, sugar, and other problem industries—suggest that adjustment might be divided into a "domestic" component and an "international" component. These compartments point to the notion that trade relief should deal exclusively with the "international" component of adjustment, namely the loss of employment

6. This summary description of the steel industry is based on Crandall (1986).

owing to rising imports; other programs (for example JTPA) should deal with the "domestic" component of adjustment.

Once an industry is designated as trade-impacted, however, it would be very troublesome to differentiate *benefits paid* as between workers who are laid off because of declining demand or fast-growing productivity, and workers who are laid-off because of rising imports. If 10,000 workers are laid off, it may be possible to make a statistical estimate that 6,000 lost their jobs because of falling demand, 2,000 because of rising productivity, and 2,000 because of higher imports. But individual workers cannot easily be assigned to those categories. Thus, the benefits paid to an individual worker or an individual firm should not depend on whether particular plant closings originated from "domestic" or "international" causes.

On the other hand, benefits might be *funded* from "domestic" sources to the extent of falling domestic demand or rising productivity, and from "international" sources to the extent of rising imports. This division of the funding burden could be carried out by an appropriate blend of general revenues, product taxes, and tariffs (or auctioned quotas). A division of the funding burden would, however, add contentious complexity to the adjustment scheme; and our calculations, reported below, suggest that tariffs (or auctioned quotas) alone would provide more than enough revenue to handle the adjustment needs of *all* departing workers and firms, whatever the cause of their exit from the industry. For these reasons, we think that the division of the funding burden between "domestic" and "international" sources should be an optional, not a mandatory, feature of the new program.

Reinvestment Policy

The proper government response to import competition should *not* entail an infusion of public capital or coerced private investment. New investment should remain the province of private initiative, undertaken only when cold calculations persuade businessmen that they can withstand the pressure of unfettered international competition.

A commendable feature of past programs of special protection is that they have seldom allocated government credit to trade-impacted industries, nor have they required impacted industries to plow back their cash flow. Under certain congressional initiatives, this hands-off feature could disappear. An early isolated example of direct government influence on the investment decisions of a trade-impacted industry was the maritime program. More recently, the Chrysler credit guarantee program, with its aura of success—resulting in large measure from subsequent trade restraints—has inspired the notion that trade protection should be tied to forced reinvestment. For example, presidential candidate Walter F. Mondale stated: "I will restrict [steel] imports for five years to give industry a chance to raise capital. [However, management must] reinvest every dollar it gets in modernization."[7] Mondale's policy prescription was echoed in section 806 of the Trade and Tariff Act of 1984.[8] Precedents have thus been established for coupling relief with reinvestment, either financed by the government (maritime and Chrysler) or forced on the industry (steel).[9]

Despite these precedents, we remain skeptical of compulsory reinvestment programs.[10] In the first place, the reinvestment approach is predicated on hope—hope for an upturn in the business cycle and hope for a technological breakthrough. In declining industries, hope can easily outrun reality. Business cycles do go up. Technological breakthroughs do happen. But the experience of Japan, Australia, the United Kingdom, Germany, and the United States suggests that phoenix stories are rare. Successful industry adjustment usually means a smaller industry and successful investment is usually aimed at downsizing, not expansion.

---

7. Bureau of National Affairs, *International Trade Reporter,* 19 September 1984, p. 296. Similar views were expressed by Stuart Eizenstat, *Washington Post,* 18 September 1984, A27.

8. Prior to the passage, on October 5, 1984, of the Trade and Tariff Act of 1984, two members of the US International Trade Commission had urged the President to make any relief to the steel industry contingent, among other things, on capital investment commitments (USITC 1984b). President Reagan's program asked the USITC to "monitor" the industry's investment decisions. See the discussion in chapter 2, section 2.2, above.

9. For a review of proposed new government institutions designed to shore up American industry, see CBO (1983, pp. 52–56).

10. The debate on the proper role of government in promoting and protecting industry can be traced to Adam Smith (1776) and Alexander Hamilton (1792). In the context of declining industries in a mature industrial society, the experience reported in the companion volume, edited by Hufbauer and Rosen, supports the views of Adam Smith. The case against compulsory reinvestment as a condition of escape clause relief is reinforced by the experience of Bethlehem Steel, which has yet to diversify and is doing far worse than the new US Steel Corporation, which has branched into petroleum and chemicals. For a contrary view, see, inter alia, Weil (1983); Labor–Industry Coalition (1983, pp. 61–64); and other sources cited in CBO (1983, p. 1).

Further, government investment programs are likely to be biased towards the most votes, not the greatest opportunities. It is not surprising that the federal government was pressured by political forces to rescue Lockheed, Conrail, and Chrysler, rather than reaching out to promote Apple Computer or MCI. Equally important, any government commitment to revive a declining industry—either using public resources or compelling private investment—can too easily pave the way for subsequent "ratification" through prolonged trade restrictions that guarantee the home market for domestic firms.[11] For 50 years, this has been the story of maritime construction subsidies. This is what happened in the Chrysler case, although it is not clear how long the industry will remain protected. And this threatens to be the story of carbon steel. When government-sponsored investment leads to trade restraints, the public pays twice and meaningful adjustment is delayed that much longer.

In our program, new investment and new research endeavors are welcome—but only when they flow from private initiative and only when private firms understand that they must ultimately meet world competition. Reliance on private investment does not mean that beleaguered industries will necessarily wither away. Very substantial cost differences separate the strongest firms from the weakest firms in every industry—footwear, autos, apparel, textiles, steel, meat, dairy, and others. With well-conceived strategies, many of the strongest firms will survive.

Adjustment Made Attractive

Relief made available under an adjustment program should be attractive by comparison with relief made available under special statutory provisions, such as section 204 of the Agricultural Act of 1956, the Magnuson Fisheries Act, or the countervailing duty and antidumping duty statutes. The tilt in favor of adjustment-oriented relief can be achieved in two ways: first by

---

11. United Auto Workers President Owen Bieber, in a speech criticizing foreign sourcing by US auto firms, outlined his vision of government's continuing role in the automobile industry: "We are willing to do our part at the collective bargaining table, but we can't assemble an overall auto policy in negotiations. Government must join with us to make such a compact work." Bieber called for the federal government to extend the VRA with Japan and to enact domestic content legislation (Bureau of National Affairs, *International Trade Reporter*, 19 September 1984, p. 324).

making other forms of relief less attractive; second by making relief with an adjustment component more attractive.

A more restrained approach to the use of constitutional and statutory powers depends on presidential resolve. This is decisive. Without presidential resolve, there can be no decline in the vices of special protection. In addition, certain statutory changes can help correct the bias that prompts distressed industries to seek relief through unfair trade laws and discretionary statutes rather than through the escape clause.[12]

The first difficulty with the escape clause is the high threshold of injury that the distressed industry must experience before qualifying for relief. Section 201 requires that imports be a "substantial cause" of actual "serious injury" or threatened serious injury. "Substantial cause" is defined as "a cause which is important and not less than any other cause."[13] In order to find serious injury, the USITC must find:

. . . the significant idling of productive facilities in the industry, the inability of a significant number of firms to operate at a reasonable level of profit, and a significant unemployment or underemployment within the industry.

Finding the threat of serious injury requires:

. . . a decline in sales, a higher and growing inventory, and a downward trend in production, profits, and wages, or employment (or increasing underemployment) in the domestic industry concerned.

---

12. Over recent decades, the dimensions of "unfair" trade have been enlarged, both by the growth of government involvement in national economies and by the wider definition of subsidy and dumping practices. As a result, many foreign trade practices can be addressed under either the "unfair" or the "fair" trade statutes. The remedies are quite different. The countervailing and antidumping duty laws presuppose that *ad hoc* US trade barriers should last as long as the offending foreign practice remains in place. By contrast, escape clause relief presupposes that *ad hoc* US trade barriers are temporary and that the domestic industry should adjust to foreign competition.

Remedies against unfair trade play an important role in providing discipline for the international trading system. The misuse of unfair trade statutes arises when remedies designed to offset precisely the amount of foreign subsidy, or the margin of dumping, are replaced by indefinite QRs (as in carbon steel or textiles) that make no reference to the extent or duration of unfair trade.

13. The GATT Article XIX test requires that imports "cause or threaten serious injury," a test that is silent as to the degree of causation required. Some scholars have argued that the GATT test requires that imports *alone* cause serious injury; others contend that they merely be *a* cause of serious injury. The US statute announces a standard between these two extremes.

The escape clause injury tests are decidedly more stringent than the injury tests applied under the unfair trade laws, namely that imports be *a* cause (not necessarily the most important cause) of actual or threatened "material injury." Material injury is simply defined as more than *de minimis* injury. Obviously, this is a far lower standard than the "substantial cause" of "serious injury" required for escape clause relief. Similarly, the escape clause injury test is decidedly more stringent than the injury tests applied under section 22 of the Agricultural Adjustment Act of 1933, section 204 of the Agricultural Act of 1956, and similar discretionary statutes.[14]

In order to make the escape clause more attractive, the gap between its injury test and the tests applied under other statutes should be narrowed. The unfair trade law test and the tests applied in special statutes are not likely to be raised. It seems far more plausible to lower the threshold for escape clause relief. An appropriate standard might be that imports "contributed importantly" to serious injury. This revision would leave the requisite degree of injury unchanged ("serious injury") but would lower the causation test ("contributed importantly" rather than "substantial cause"). The "contributed importantly" test is already embodied in the Trade Adjustment Assistance (TAA) law.[15] Under this approach, if the industry were seriously harmed, and if imports contributed importantly to the industry's ills, but were not necessarily the most important cause, the industry would be eligible for escape clause relief.[16]

A second reason that firms prefer to seek relief under the unfair trade laws or through special statutes, rather than through the escape clause, is that escape clause relief can be denied by the President for a variety of reasons.[17]

---

14. For example, under section 22, the President may issue an emergency proclamation increasing duties by 50 percent or decreasing quantities imported by 50 percent: "Whenever the Secretary of Agriculture has reason to believe that any article or articles are being or are practically certain to be imported into the United States under such conditions and in such quantities as to render or tend to render ineffective, or materially interfere with, any program or operation undertaken [by the Department of Agriculture]." Nonemergency section 22 cases are referred to the USITC for an injury determination under the same relaxed test.

15. Section 222 of the Trade Act of 1974 states: "the term 'contributed importantly' means a cause that is important but not necessarily more important than any other cause."

16. If the industry were seriously harmed by circumstances other than imports, an adjustment program might still be designed to deal with its difficulties. However, the program would not contain import restraint elements.

17. The laundry list of presidential criteria appears in section 202 of the Trade Act of 1974.

By contrast, countervailing duty and antidumping duty relief are granted by administrative decision; and the President must answer to powerful congressional committees when he alters the relief available under special statutes.

We propose to make the escape clause a more certain remedy by conferring on the US International Trade Commission sole power to grant or deny escape clause relief.[18] In our plan, the President, speaking through the US Trade Representative (USTR), would play the decisive role in deciding what *form* relief would take, not the *grant* of relief. We support this feature as it appears in numerous pieces of legislation currently being discussed on the Hill. Further, an industry that received escape clause relief would *not* simultaneously be eligible for unfair trade remedies and vice versa.[19] The argument for requiring petitioning industries to make an election is that either escape clause relief or unfair trade relief can adequately address the trade-related injury experienced by the industry. Thus, the industry should choose whether to pursue remedies of indefinite duration, designed to offset foreign unfair trade practices, or whether to pursue time-limited remedies, designed to enable the industry to meet the vagaries of international competition.

All in all, these changes in eligibility criteria would undoubtedly add to the frequency and volume of escape clause relief. At the same time they should decidedly subtract from trade relief granted through other means of special protection.

US International Trade Commission Role

The USITC would continue to play its customary role in defining the boundaries of the trade-impacted industry and in determining whether the requisite degree and causation of injury exists. In addition, the USITC would have several new tasks.

---

18. The Heinz bill (S 1863), originally introduced in 1983, suggested a similar change. In our plan, the Commission's decisions could be appealed for review by the Court of International Trade, under a standard that requires the appellant to show clear and convincing error by the Commission.

19. The reference here to unfair trade remedies includes only antidumping duty and countervailing duty relief. The industry could, for example, simultaneously seek relief under section 301 of the Trade Act of 1974 (to reduce unfair barriers to foreign markets) and relief under the escape clause.

First, the USITC would determine the extent to which rising imports contribute to the industry's injury by comparison with other factors—falling demand at home, rising productivity, and loss of export markets. The relative extent of import-related injury would be expressed in terms of the adverse impact on the volume and price of goods sold and the level of employment. This information would be forwarded to the USTR for guidance in selecting a relief package, and it would be made publicly available to promote informed discussion. However, as mentioned earlier, the analytical division between "domestic" and "international" causes of injury would not compel a parallel funding burden between "domestic" and "international" sources of revenue.

The USITC would work with the Department of Labor, the Department of Commerce, and the Department of Agriculture (as appropriate) to design the adjustment programs. The USITC would spell out the pace at which protection and assistance would be reduced. In other words, the USITC would design and coordinate both the adjustment and the relief side of the program, subject to statutory guidelines.

Based on data supplied by the petitioning industry, the appropriate department would establish an inventory of workers, capital, and farmland engaged in the industry as of a defined date, the "inventory date." Eligibility for adjustment assistance would be conditioned, as a preliminary test, on the physical presence of the factors in the industry on the inventory date.[20] After the inventory date is past, new workers, new capital, and new land would enter the industry at their own risk. New entrants would *not* be eligible for assistance, apart from whatever temporary benefits are conferred from serving a protected domestic market.[21]

Second, the USITC, after consultation with the appropriate departments, would establish eligibility criteria (within statutory guidelines) for early retirement, retraining, and relocation benefits for workers, cash assistance to firms, and cash payments to farmers (more on these subjects later).

---

20. In the case of previously laid-off and still unemployed workers, their presence in the industry six months prior to the inventory date could meet the test.

21. Once the industry weathered a significant period, say ten years, without protection or other USITC assistance, then all firms and workers would again be eligible for USITC relief. This waiting period is designed to avoid two dangers: the creation of a revolving door program dispensing on-budget benefits to workers; and the creation of new firms that first take advantage of short-term protection provided to existing firms, and then seek a new round of relief.

Third, the USITC could confer limited antitrust immunity for firms to meet and discuss plant closures, and to arrange side payments between firms that remained open and firms that closed their plants. In other words, the USITC would provide a forum for firms to pursue cooperative adjustment approaches to the more permanent alternative of merger. If firms wished to merge, they would still need prior approval of the Justice Department (or risk litigation under the Clayton Act). This proposal does not go as far as the Reagan administration proposals, which could promote too much leeway in determining antitrust policy.

As its fourth task, the USITC would calculate the amount and time profile of public and private resources needed for the envisaged relief and adjustment programs, taking into account the benefits of limited antitrust immunity. The USITC would then prepare a menu of funding alternatives that meet the calculated needs. Each alternative would be structured to provide, as nearly as possible, the same quantum of relief, and to require the same pace of adjustment by the domestic industry. However, the alternative approaches would differ radically in terms of relative burden imposed on domestic and foreign suppliers, the use of the price mechanism to ration imports, and the extent to which assistance is provided through off-budget or on-budget means.[22] The choice between these alternatives involves important policy considerations, with far-reaching domestic and international repercussions. Thus the method of funding relief and the collateral consequences for trade policy would be determined by the US Trade Representative in consultation with other executive branch agencies, the House Ways and Means Committee, and the Senate Finance Committee.

The four basic components that the USITC would draw on in designing alternative funding programs would include:

- a tariff on imports of the product; or quantitative restrictions on imports with quota rights auctioned by the US Treasury; in both cases with the proceeds earmarked (to the extent necessary) to assist the industry[23]

---

22. Historically, in a wide range of circumstances, the United States has preferred off-budget means of assisting industries (CBO 1984, p. 77). On-budget assistance may be far more desirable from the standpoint of efficiency and transparency, but it commands a far smaller political constituency.

23. The idea of converting quotas to tariffs or auctioned quotas and dedicating the revenues to adjustment purposes has been advocated by Bhagwati (1982); Hufbauer and Rosen (1983); and Schultz and Schumacher (1984), among others.

• quantitative restraints on imports, either allocated to the domestic import-competing industry or assigned to individual exporting countries; with worker and firm adjustment programs funded either by the industry or by general budget receipts

• a special tax on the product, levied *both* on domestic production and on imports (and rebated on exports), with the proceeds used to assist the industry[24]

• the use of general budget revenues to finance adjustment, with no import restraints.

For each funding alternative, the USITC would draw up tables relating projected resources generated to levels of tax, tariff, or quota restraints. The extent of any trade protection would be scheduled by the USITC to decline by a regular amount each year, enough to phase out protection over a five-year period. Likewise, the quantum of support financed by public revenues (or by industry contributions to a pool) would decline year by year.

After the USTR selected an approach from the menu of relief options, the USITC would hold periodic hearings (for example, every three years) to determine whether the scheduled rate of degressive protection or income support should be modified, taking into account the pace of adjustment and whether the flow of earmarked public funds or industry-financed programs was adequate.

The program initially selected by USTR might not generate adequate resources—through taxes, tariffs, designated general revenues, or otherwise—for the relief and adjustment program prescribed by the USITC. If the resource shortfall exceeded statutory guidelines (say by a margin of 20 percent from the initial projections), the USITC would be required to redesign the program. The redesigned program would entail higher product taxes, higher tariffs, smaller quotas, or reduced relief payments per departing worker. In the meantime, the funding deficiency would be paid through general revenues. The redesigned program, like the original program, would contemplate degressive protection over time.

---

24. Taxes of this sort have been widely used in US agricultural programs, for example in the Jones–Costigan Act of 1934 that regulated sugar production and imports.

Conversely, in the happy (but not unusual) event that resources exceed the relief needs of the industry,[25] the USITC would be called upon to redesign the program to prescribe lower taxes or tariffs or larger quotas.

US Trade Representative Role

The USTR, in consultation with other executive branch agencies, the House Ways and Means Committee, and the Senate Finance Committee, would assemble a program from the relief menu designed by the USITC. The design of the program would thus reflect the policy concerns of other executive agencies and the key congressional committees.

In choosing among program alternatives, the USTR and its policy colleagues would decide between relief measures that entail more or less budget expenditure; relief measures that involve more or less protection; relief measures that prompt larger or smaller requests by foreign countries for "compensation" or "retaliation"; relief measures that distribute greater benefits to prosperous firms and fewer benefits to not so prosperous firms, or vice versa; and relief measures that place the burden on consumers or the public at large.

The pull and haul between these choices already goes on whenever special protection is debated. In today's policy context, however, the choice is often deflected into avenues that involve no relief for the industry (as with copper) or indefinite off-budget protection (as with steel). These two avenues, as they currently exist, would no longer be available.

Several observations can be made about the choices that prospectively face the USTR and its policy colleagues. By statute, the USTR would give weight to the USITC determination as to the extent of import-related injury in fashioning the relief program. By statutory presumption, protection would be a less important part of the program if import-related injury was a less important part of total injury, but this presumption would not bind the USTR. In addition, the USTR would consider the adjustment measures undertaken by other countries. If the products in question were exported predominantly by countries with effective adjustment programs of their own, and if other

---

25. The hypothetical adjustment calculations summarized in tables 5.1 to 5.3 suggest that resources raised through tariffs and quota auctions alone would often exceed the relief needs of troubled industries.

important importing countries also subscribed to the adjustment philosophy, the USTR would properly rely to a lesser degree on protection.

The role of protection in the relief and adjustment program would be concretely determined by the choice of policy instruments. The burden on foreign producers would be greatest with straight tariffs or auctioned quotas and least with assistance financed by general budget receipts or by a product tax. A product tax would be most appropriate if imports were small and the impact of imports barely exceeded the requisite injury threshhold. The use of quantitative restraints, such as VRAs and VERs, that assigned import rights to foreign producers, would impose an intermediate burden on foreign producers: their loss from smaller volumes exported to the United States would be partly offset by their economic rents derived from preferential access to the controlled US market.

The USTR would also consider the budget aspects. A product tax or general revenues would provide assistance in an entirely on-budget manner— that is to say, the benefits provided to the domestic industry would entirely pass through the public purse. By contrast, a tariff or quota auction would be semi-budget—the protective benefits to the domestic industry resulting from higher product prices would be off-budget, but the tariff and quota revenues would be on-budget, although directly allocated to finance adjustment. Finally, allocated quotas would be entirely off-budget—both the protective effect, and any adjustment scheme put together by the domestic industry, would occur outside of normal budget channels.

Certain approaches have special attributes. For example, industry contributions to an adjustment pool would make more sense for a concentrated industry of large firms, such as autos, than for a competitive industry of small firms, such as dairy products. As an illustration, in the case of autos, the Big Three US manufacturers might be required to earmark a significant portion of their VRA and VER profits for early retirement and worker retraining programs.

The allocation of import rights to existing domestic producers would provide no compensation to foreign producers, but would facilitate the transition of domestic firms from a manufacturing to a distributing role. This method has been used to good advantage in the United Kingdom, particularly for consumer electronics.

The use of a product tax would be most appropriate when product demand is inelastic, as for sugar. Indeed, the Agricultural Adjustment Act of 1933 was designed with just such taxes in mind. By contrast, the use of general revenues would be most appropriate when imports are a modest cause of injury and demand is highly elastic.

In addition to selecting a program, the USTR would be assigned statutory authority for dealing with the compensation and retaliation issues, again subject to consultation with other executive branch agencies and the key congressional committees. Postwar reliance on selective quantitative restrictions has diminished the role of customary compensation and retaliation as envisaged in the GATT.[26] Our program envisages a rediscovery of the compensation requirements of GATT Article XIX. Four main choices would be available to the USTR:

• The USTR could provide compensation through the use of orderly marketing agreements (OMAs) or voluntary restraint agreements (VRAs) in which quota rights are assigned to the affected foreign countries. This method (or a close variant) is quite often used today. One major problem is that it provides no budget resources for domestic adjustment. Another problem is that this method abets discriminatory, non-MFN, safeguards.

• The USTR could acquiesce in directional low-rate tariffs imposed by affected foreign countries on all US exports. In other words, the United States would selectively waive its GATT rights to most-favored-nation treatment for the limited purpose of creating a compensation fund. The proceeds of directional tariffs would be used (at the exporting country's discretion) to assist the impacted local industry. This would be a new method of meeting the compensation requirements of GATT Article XIX.

• The USTR could liberalize specific US tariffs. This method, though rarely used, is contemplated both in Article XIX of the GATT and in section 123 of the Trade Act of 1974.

• The USTR could accede to the suspension of "substantially equivalent concessions" on particular US products. This method is contemplated in GATT Article XIX and is occasionally used today.

• In the context of a new Safeguards Code, the USTR could ask affected countries to waive their compensation rights, in consideration of the domestic

---

26. A GATT study (5 July 1978, annex D) indicates that, out of 84 safeguard actions taken by contracting parties between 1950 and 1977, compensation was granted in only 19 instances and retaliation occurred only four times. However, as noted in chapter 2 a good deal of informal compensation takes place through the assignment of quota rights to affected exporters when selective QRs are applied.

US adjustment program and in contemplation of future cases in which the affected countries would implement their own adjustment programs free of compensation claims by the United States. This would represent a new approach.

Worker Assistance

Neither retraining nor relocation offers a magical solution for the displaced worker. No program can guarantee to an unemployed Monongahela Valley steel worker that, by moving to the Sunbelt, or by retraining for a year, he will gain a new job at the prevailing wage rate in the steel industry. But the proper comparison is not between the status quo and retraining or relocation; in troubled industries, production jobs will decline under almost all foreseeable trade regimes. Thus the proper comparison is between income maintenance (often at meager levels) and retraining or relocation. Whatever their weaknesses—and they are many—retraining and relocation offer a better opportunity for new employment than income maintenance that requires no effort by the employee.

In our plan, the USITC, in consultation with the Department of Labor, would design retraining, relocation, and early retirement programs, subject to statutory guidelines.[27] Eligibility would be conditioned both on the worker's presence in the industry on the inventory date and on the worker's prior connection with the industry (for example, eligibility might require an aggregate period of employment of at least three years). Financing would be provided either through public funds—derived from tariffs, auctioned quotas, product taxes, or general revenues—or through industry contributions to a pool operated for the benefit of all employees.

Statutory maximum benefits for retraining might be limited to 65 percent of the employee's prior wage plus retraining costs, for a period up to 18 months.[28] To promote meaningful retraining, a voucher approach would be

27. For a review of programs that are currently available, largely administered by the Department of Labor, see CBO (1982).

28. Under existing law, over the period 1975–82, the average TAA payment per worker was only $2,941 (USTR 1984, p. 150). Similarly, under a 1983 contract between the Communications Workers and AT&T, the company will provide up to $2,500 per worker for job training and relocation (Choate, Carey, and Lovell 1984, p. 4). Our program is designed to be substantially more generous, but the costs would still be less than the costs of special protection. As a matter of interest, the French government has enjoyed considerable success with programs that provide retraining and 70 percent replacement wages for up to 10 months (*Wall Street Journal*, 6 November 1984, p. 32).

used, and on-the-job training would qualify as an accredited program. Adequate job search and relocation allowances would be made available.[29] In addition, the USITC would specify limits on qualified job search and retraining costs, paid by employees out of their own resources, that would qualify for an income tax deduction. The statutory minimum age for early retirement might be 60, with early retirement benefits not exceeding 65 percent of the employee's prior wage lasting up to five years. Within such statutory guidelines, the USITC would design programs for individual industries.

First preference for early retirement, retraining, and relocation funds would be given to applicants already laid-off in the industry. Other workers could volunteer for program benefits. Program benefits for volunteers would, however, be limited to planned resources, without tapping general budget revenues beyond planned levels.

Industrial Plant and Farmland

The USITC, in consultation with the Department of Commerce, would design programs to help finance adjustment by firms, again subject to statutory guidelines. The finance would come either from public funds generated by tariffs, quota auctions, or other earmarked sources, or plant-closing agreements negotiated between firms in the industry.

Public funds would be used to purchase, at face value, the tax loss carryforwards generated by plant closings. This approach would ensure that public funds are only paid to corporate groups that experience losses throughout their operations, since profitable groups would absorb internally the tax losses generated by individual divisions.

There would be two further conditions of eligibility. First, plant and equipment would have to be converted to other uses, exported, or scrapped. This test is designed to avoid the use of program resources to recycle physical capital back into the same industry. Second, the firm would have to spend the funds received on new investment, not on merging with an existing tax-paying firm.[30]

---

29. Under present law, the maximum for job search and relocation allowances combined is $1,600 plus 90 percent of out-of-pocket relocation expenses (USTR 1984, p. 149).

30. A firm that wished to combine with an existing taxpaying firm would presumably realize the *market* value of its tax loss carryforwards in the acquisition or merger. Based on experience with "safe-harbor" leasing, the market value is substantially less than the face value.

In consultation with the Department of Agriculture, the USITC would design farmland programs. Benefits to farmland would be conditioned on a restrictive covenant not to grow the particular crop, or not to husband the particular animals, on farmland once used for that purpose.[31] The decision to enroll farmland in the program would be entirely voluntary with farm owners. The program would establish acreage fees for covenants to retire farmland for a specified term of years. Depending on the program, farmland retired from a particular use might be available for all other uses, or might, as with Soil Bank and Payment-in-Kind programs, be retired from all commercial agricultural production.[32]

Because so much farm labor is either associated with farm ownership or is highly seasonal, we do not envisage a large program for farm workers. However, farm workers (other than farm owners) who had spent more than a specified amount of work time on the trade-impacted crops for more than a certain number of years (say 100 working days a year for three years) would be eligible for early retirement, retraining, and relocation benefits. In addition, employees and firms in trade-impacted processing industries, such as sugar mills and dairy processing, would be eligible for the normal range of benefits.

Existing Special Protection

Parallel steps should be taken to unwind existing cases of special protection. Existing cases may, however, require custom tailoring, because entire industries and regions have come to depend on federal barriers to foreign competition. In some cases, adjustment has been postponed so long that a wide chasm separates the US industry from its foreign competitors.

The adjustment process in existing cases should be initiated by a request from the USTR directing the USITC to design degressive relief measures. The USTR request would be made only after consultation with other executive branch agencies and key congressional committees. The menu of degressive remedies would be much the same as for new escape clause cases. Among

---

31. Eligibility tests would be framed in terms of use of the farmland for the particular crop on the inventory date and during a specified prior period (say three of the past five years).

32. The concept of farmland set-asides was introduced by the Agricultural Adjustment Act of 1938 (which provided for voluntary and mandatory acreage controls). It was extended in the Soil Bank program introduced in the Agricultural Act of 1956, and most recently applied in the 1983 payment-in-kind (PIK) program.

other options, the menu would include limited antitrust immunity and programs designed to convert existing quantitative restrictions into tariffs or auctioned quotas, with the revenues used to finance adjustment. However, the phase-out horizon might be longer than for new cases, because the starting level of protection is higher. As a working assumption, we would project a 1 percent to 3 percent decrease a year in tariff or tariff-equivalent protection. In industries like apparel and dairy, where the tariff equivalent of protection probably exceeds 40 percent, the phase-out might require 15 years or more.

The US decision to implement adjustment programs in existing cases of special protection would very likely be conditioned on similar pledges from Japan, Europe, Canada, and advanced developing countries such as Brazil and Mexico. Japan, for example, might inaugurate an adjustment program for its rice, beef, and citrus farmers in the context of an American automobile program and a European textile program. International commitments would be phrased in terms of several goals: a specified reduction of protective barriers; a specified growth in the market share held by imports; and minimum and maximum rates of exit of workers, plant capacity, and farmland. Within these commitments, each country should be free to develop its own adjustment programs.

In the case of existing programs of special protection that spring from statutory relief schemes, the USTR choice of an alternative adjustment program would require the "fast-track" approval of Congress.[33] This would apply, for example, to relief under section 204 of the Agricultural Act of 1956, section 22 of the Agricultural Adjustment Act of 1933, the Meat Act, the Jones Act, and so forth. "Fast-track" review would give Congress an opportunity to consider the views of affected constituents, to examine reciprocal international concessions, and to exercise its constitutional role in regulating foreign commerce.

Illustrative Examples

The United States could certainly do worse than its present approach to special protection. But the United States could also do much better. As a

---

33. The "fast-track" approval process was devised in the Trade Act of 1974. Under this process, the President gives Congress 90 days notification prior to submitting legislation; Congress then votes on the legislation, without amendment, within 60 days after submission. In many cases, "fast-track" approval would answer political sensitivities, even if not required to alter relief under the applicable statute.

way of illustrating the better alternative, we have prepared numerical examples of possible adjustment programs that might replace existing cases of special protection. These examples are summarized in tables 5.1, 5.2, and 5.3 (Hufbauer, Berliner, and Elliott 1986; Bergsten and Hufbauer 1985).

In the examples, rough assumptions were made about various parameters—consumption growth, productivity growth, elasticities of demand, and so forth. The programs are designed to adjust resources unemployed *both* from "international" and from "domestic" causes. Protection is scheduled to decline at 1 to 3 percentage points per year, expressed in tariff-equivalent terms. All in all, the adjustment programs do not entail a marked increase in the rate of labor or acreage exit, or the pace of import penetration, by comparison with recent experience.

Employment in the troubled industries is projected to decline, generally by 2 percent to 5 percent annually. This is about the same as past experience in these industries. Less than half the decline is associated with imports. The rest stems from "domestic" causes. The adjustment programs would, of course, cover workers, farmland, and livestock no matter why they are dislocated.

The share of the domestic market supplied by imports rises about 1 percent to 3 percent a year under the hypothetical programs. Again, this is about the same as past experience with troubled industries.

The programs envisage large on-budget, self-financed payments to the workers and firms that face the burden of adjustment. We assumed, as an arbitrary but high estimate, that overall costs of the program would work out to *twice* the average annual wage of each separated worker. This figure includes allowances for early retirement, retraining, relocation, and industry adjustment. Wage costs are estimated in the range of $15,000 to $36,000 per separated worker a year. Thus, adjustment costs are calculated in the $30,000 to $72,000 per worker range. This is very much larger than the average TAA benefit per worker, which peaked at $7,000 in 1981 (USTR p. 150), but is substantially less than the consumer costs per job "saved" of existing import protection. Similarly, the cost for retiring farmland was set at $1,000 to $1,500 an acre, and the cost for retiring livestock at $500 to $600 a head. We have deliberately set high cost figures, both to make the new program attractive by comparison with special protection and to allow for a margin of error in the number of workers (or acres or livestock) receiving assistance.

We assumed that quantitative restraints would either be converted to tariffs or sold as auctioned quotas. On this assumption, it appears possible to fund

5.1 Characteristics of hypothetical adjustment programs, 17 industries

Case	Employment[a]				Import market share			Program cost	
	1984[b] (thousand)	1990[b] (thousand)	Annual change due to domestic factors[c] (percentage)	Annual change due to rising import share (percentage)	1984 (percentage)	1990 (percentage)	Annual change 1990 (percentage points)	Assumed adjustment cost per worker[b] (dollars)	Net budgetary surplus (cost) of adjustment program[d] (million dollars)
Manufacturing									
M–1 Book Manufacturing	33	22	–3.0	–2.5	20.0	32.0	2.0	24,000	(199)
M–3 Glassware	12	10	–1.9	–1.2	23.0	30.0	1.2	20,000	185
M–4 Rubber Footwear	15	10	–1.0	–5.2	64.0	76.0	2.0	17,000	744
M–5 Ceramic Articles	8	6	–1.9	–2.3	66.0	71.4	0.9	17,000	306
M–6 Ceramic Tiles	6	5	–1.9	–0.9	48.7	52.1	0.6	17,000	191
M–7 Orange Juice	4	4	2.1	–2.8	30.0	41.0	1.8	17,000	944
M–8 Canned Tuna	13	11	–1.9	–0.6	15.7	19.9	0.7	16,000	(35)
M–11 Textiles and Apparel: Phase III	1,980	1,696	–1.0	–1.4	20.4	27.7	1.2	17,500	15,210
M–14 Carbon Steel: Phase III	170	128	–3.3	–0.8	26.7	25.5	–0.2	35,000	15,223
M–16 Specialty Steel	14	10	–4.2	–1.1	16.4	23.6	1.2	35,000	35
M–22 Automobiles	605	460	–2.7	–1.3	33.7	41.9	1.4	35,000	6,100

Services								
S–1 Maritime Industries	14	8	–2.6	–4.8	65.0	77.0	2.0	36,000	11,131
Agriculture and Fisheries								
A–1 Sugar	20	12	–0.2	–6.8	37.4	57.1	3.3	15,000	158
	1,800	1,100	–0.2	–6.2				1,000/acre	
	(acres)	(acres)							
A–2 Dairy Products	94	69	–3.5	–0.9	4.3	10.2	1.0	15,000	557
	11,100	8,700	–2.7	–0.9				600/cow	
	(cows)	(cows)							
A–3 Peanuts	1,400	1,310	0.0	–1.1	neg.	6.2	1.0	1,500/acre	(110)
	(acres)	(acres)							
A–4 Meat	168	140	–1.9	–0.9	6.0	12.0	1.0	20,000	(259)
	114,000	114,000	0.9	–0.9				500/head	
	(head)	(head)							
A–5 Fish	200	216	2.5	1.3	60.0	62.5	0.4	15,000	770

Neg. Negligible.

a. The annual changes due to productivity and consumption growth and rising import share are based on figures to be found in the cases. The net effect on employment as derived from the percentage figures may not agree with the percentage change derived from employment figures in this table since these have been rounded to the nearest thousand.

b. All figures, unless otherwise specified, refer to workers in the industry.

c. These are changes due to increases in productivity and consumption growth.

d. These figures represent the net budgetary surplus (outlay) of the hypothetical adjustment programs over the period 1985–90.

the envisaged levels of assistance without using product taxes or general budget receipts. This result reflects the recapture of very high quota rents that are now garnered by private foreign suppliers and US importers. Nevertheless, in the spirit of dividing the funding burden between "domestic" and "international" causes of decline, and as a matter of international comity, in many instances part of the program could be funded with general revenues and product taxes.

The Current Debate

Many of our recommendations are echoed in the Trade Adjustment Assistance Reform and Extension Act of 1985 (S 1544), sponsored by Senators William V. Roth (R-Del.) and Daniel Patrick Moynihan (D-NY). This legislation calls for up to a 1 percent across-the-board tariff on all imports, with proceeds used to finance adjustment. The actual adjustment aspect of the program would grant each worker a $4,000 job retraining voucher redeemable for training, and condition all cash benefits to workers on enrollment in some form of training program.

There are several key similarities between our proposal and the Roth-Moynihan approach:

- Both would generate *new* revenue from trade flows themselves.

- Both would dedicate the trade-generated revenue to TAA, with any excess used to reduce the overall budget deficit.

- Both envisage voucher systems for retraining.

- Both would seek international acceptance of the new approach in light of existing GATT commitments and the need for innovative adjustment approaches in the new round of international trade talks.

At the same time, there are several significant differences between the proposals. Ours would generate and use trade-related revenues on a closely matched *industry-by-industry* basis, whereas Roth-Moynihan would take an across-the-board approach. Our plan has the virtue of applying the "user cost" principle more precisely and directly, whereas the proposed legislation has the virtue of avoiding "industrial planning" on an industry-by-industry basis.

A second important difference is that our proposal would generate higher levels of additional revenue for TAA purposes: about $8.7 billion in new revenue in 1986 if the proposed conversion of QRs to tariffs were immediately carried out for all 17 industries (tables 5.2 and 5.3), as opposed to under $4

TABLE 5.2   **Gross revenues, expenditures, and net revenues of hypothetical trade adjustment programs, 17 industries[a]**
(million dollars)

	1986	1987	1988	1989	1990
Gross revenues					
Total (including existing tariffs)	15,060	14,251	12,999	11,816	10,538
New (from conversion of existing nontariff barriers [NTBs] to new tariffs or auctioned quotas)	8,703	7,493	6,674	5,893	5,089
Assumed expenditures for TAA[b]	5,355	5,166	5,055	4,742	4,520
Net surplus of hypothetical TAA program (including existing tariffs)	9,705	9,085	7,944	7,074	6,018
Net surplus from conversion of existing NTBs to new tariffs or auctioned quotas	3,348	2,327	1,619	1,151	567

a. Based on estimates in Hufbauer, Berliner, and Elliott (1986). The 17 industries are listed in table 5.1
b. Expenditures are based on twice the average annual wage of production workers in the industries. This would cover not only assistance to workers (by far the largest use of funds) but also assistance to firms and communities.

billion for Roth-Moynihan even with the maximum 1 percent tariff. Our approach could thus fund a more ambitious pace of adjustment, on humane terms, and offer a meaningful alternative to the entrenched regimes of special protection.

Third, our proposal would not increase the existing level of protection (assuming a faithful and accurate conversion of existing nontariff restraints into their tariff equivalents), whereas the Roth-Moynihan proposal would do so to a modest extent. In principle, this suggests that our approach might be more easily negotiated internationally. However, it must be recognized that our approach *would* violate existing GATT tariff bindings in a major way and thus necessitate Article XXVIII negotiations to redress any imbalance in concessions. Since there would be no net change in protection, however, and since increased transparency and greater prospects for subsequent reduction of the barriers would result, little if any compensation should actually be required. Less defensibly, some exporting countries might also

TABLE 5.3   **Net revenue surplus (deficit) of hypothetical trade adjustment programs, 17 industries[a]**
(million dollars)

Industry	1986	1987	1988	1989	1990
All from existing tariffs					
Glass products	40	34	28	25	14
Rubber footwear	130	126	123	119	113
Ceramic articles	56	52	51	47	44
Ceramic tiles	32	32	31	32	32
Orange juice	150	155	160	165	170
Canned tuna[b]	(2)	(4)	(7)	(9)	(12)
From all sources[c]					
Textiles and apparel					
Total revenues	3,145	2,945	2,350	2,005	1,580
New revenues	(1,055)	(1,565)	(1,680)	(1,575)	(1,470)
Carbon steel					
Total revenues	2,572	2,533	2,485	2,399	2,304
New revenues	2,112	2,043	1,975	1,869	1,754
Specialty steel					
Total revenues	18	12	(3)	(19)	(2)
New revenues	(30)	(41)	(53)	(49)	(28)
Automobiles					
Total revenues	1,000	1,000	900	800	600
New revenues	10	(88)	(257)	(450)	(720)
Meat					
Total revenues	(6)	(19)	(43)	(72)	(117)
New revenues	(63)	(84)	(116)	(153)	(176)
Fisheries					
Total revenues	230	160	80	—	—
New revenues	115	80	40		
All from new revenues					
Book manufacturing	(60)	(44)	(31)	27	(14)
Maritime	2,301	1,989	1,688	1,402	1,124
Sugar	71	45	50	10	4
Dairy products	46	90	100	160	191
Peanuts	(20)	(18)	(18)	(17)	(17)

a. Based on estimates in Hufbauer, Berliner, and Elliott (1986).

b. These figures are based on the assumption that the over-quota and under-quota tariff rates on canned tuna are consolidated. See Case M–8, Canned Tuna, in Hufbauer, Berliner, and Elliott (1986).

c. Existing tariffs and converted quantitative restraints (either auctioned quotas or tariffs).

object to giving up the rents that they now obtain from the present technique of allocating quotas to foreign governments and thereafter to individual suppliers. However, we regard this transfer of resources to the United States from Japan, Korea, and other exporting countries as an important benefit of the scheme, and as the principal means of funding adjustment.

Fourth, our proposal goes beyond the Senate version in suggesting new techniques for promoting adjustment and providing more generous benefits for both workers and firms. By easing the criterion for injury determination and expanding the benefits to workers, our goal is to induce firms and workers to accept the downsizing that seems required in virtually all adjustment cases.

As mentioned in chapter 3, the existing Trade Adjustment Assistance (TAA) program officially expired on December 19, 1985. Congress extended appropriations for previously certified workers in two continuing resolutions at the end of 1985. In one of the final acts of the 1985 session, Congress removed TAA cash benefits from its final continuing resolution, thus continuing funding only for job search, retraining, and relocation benefits.

The House and Senate budget reconciliation bill, which is required before any program changes can be made in the budget, includes the Roth-Moynihan import surcharge adjustment reforms. Congress must now either (1) reauthorize the existing TAA program and appropriate the necessary funds to continue cash benefits, (2) accept the House-Senate budget reconciliation bill and make the necessary appropriations, or (3) pass new legislation reinstating TAA. The final budget hurdle is the Gramm–Rudman–Hollings law, that dictates across-the-board budget cuts in order to reduce the overall budget deficit. Nevertheless, the prospects for legislation in 1986 look good as Congress searches for responsible answers to protectionist pressure (Cooper 1986). However, any congressional action must be approved by the President.

Danger of Misdirected Action

How would the new approach work in practice? Everything depends on the ability of Congress and the President to carry out their contemplated roles. Our era is highly skeptical about public efforts to improve the workings of the private economy. In the context of trade adjustment, the danger of misdirected action seems particularly strong because foreign producers are not represented in the American political system. One scenario will illustrate the dangers.

Before it emerged from Congress, the new statute might be subtly converted into a blueprint for indefinite protection. Degressive protection would become an *option*, not a *requirement*.[34] Publicly supported investment programs, designed to reinvigorate the industry, would be another option. Then, as the program was administered, political forces would predictably converge on the revival option. When new technology and new equipment could not meet foreign competition, a new cycle of protection would begin. Under this scenario, additional industries might come to resemble the US merchant marine and the US sugar industry, insulated from foreign competition by a web of protection and subsidies. The present approach of "grudging concession" to the advocates of special protection might well look like a golden era compared with this outcome.

Other unfortunate scenarios can be sketched. For example, the USTR might continue to resort to OMAs rather than exploring alternatives such as tariffs, quota auctions, and product taxes; the USTR might use its negotiating authority to fashion government-sponsored cartels (as in carbon steel, textiles, and dairy) rather than to open markets; the USITC might use periodic reviews to postpone indefinitely the reduction of tariffs, taxes, and income support; and Congress might see the new program as a supplement rather than a substitute for existing means of providing special protection.

The danger of misdirected action stalks every proposal for government intervention. We believe that misdirection is not inevitable. But we also believe that perverse results can only be avoided if the Congress and the President explicitly embrace the four concepts listed in the left column, rather than the four concepts listed in the right column:

Embrace	*Reject*
Degressive protection	Indefinite protection
Limited industry support	Open-ended industry support
Public assistance to downsize the industry	Public investment to revive the industry
Competition in international markets	Quasi-cartels in international markets

Over the past 30 years, special protection has insidiously become the American blend of trade policy and industrial policy. It is time to try a different approach.

---

34. The distinction between predictably degressive protection as an *option* or as a *requirement* lies at the heart of the current debate over industrial policy.

Bibliography

This bibliography lists only general reference works, including but not limited to items referenced in the text. Materials dealing with individual instances of US protection and adjustment are listed in Hufbauer, Berliner, and Elliott (1986).

Aho, C. Michael, and Thomas O. Bayard. 1980. "American Trade Adjustment Assistance after Five Years." *The World Economy,* vol. 3, no. 4 (December).

———. 1984a. "Costs and Benefits of Trade Adjustment Assistance." Discussion paper for the Study Group on US Trade and Adjustment Policy, Council on Foreign Relations. Washington, 27 February.

———. 1984b. "Costs and Benefits of Trade Adjustment Assistance." In *The Structure and Evolution of Recent US Trade Policy.* Edited by Robert Baldwin and Anne O. Krueger. National Bureau of Economic Research Conference Report. Chicago: University of Chicago Press.

Aho, C. Michael, and James Orr. 1981. "Trade-Sensitive Employment: Who Are the Affected Workers?" *Monthly Labor Review,* vol. 104, no. 2 (February).

American Enterprise Institute. 1983. "Reauthorization of Trade Adjustment Assistance." AEI Legislative Analyses. Washington, September.

Anderson, Kym, and Robert E. Baldwin. 1981. "The Political Market for Protection in Industrial Countries: Empirical Evidence." World Bank Staff Working Paper, no. 492. Washington, October.

Bailey, Pat (Federal Trade Commission). 1984. "The Perils of Protectionism." Charles Francis Adams Lecture, Fletcher School of Law and Diplomacy, Medford, Mass., October.

Balassa, Bela, and Carol Balassa. 1984. "Industrial Protection in the Developed Countries." *The World Economy,* vol. 7, no. 2 (June).

Baldwin, Robert E. 1984a. "The Political Economy of US Import Policy." University of Wisconsin, Madison, October.

———. 1984b. "Rent-seeking and Trade Policy: An Industry Approach." University of Wisconsin, Madison, October.

Baldwin, Robert·E., and Anne O. Krueger, eds. 1984. *The Structure and Evolution of Recent US Trade Policy.* National Bureau of Economic Research Conference Report. Chicago: University of Chicago Press.

Bale, Malcolm D. 1974. "Adjustment Assistance under the Trade Expansion Act of 1962." *Journal of International Law and Economics,* vol. 9.

———. 1979. "Adjustment Assistance: Dealing with Import-Displaced Workers." In *Tariffs, Quotas and Trade: The Politics of Protectionism.* San Francisco: Institute for Contemporary Studies.

95

Bale, Malcolm D., and Ulrich Koester. 1983. "Maginot Line of European Farm Policies." *The World Economy*, vol. 6, no. 4 (December).

Baranson, Jack. 1981. *The Japanese Challenge to US Industry*. Lexington, Mass.: D. C. Heath and Co.

Bauer, Raymond A., Ithiel de Sola Pool, and Lewis Anthony Dexter. 1972. *American Business and Public Policy: The Politics of Foreign Trade*. 2d ed. Chicago: Aldine-Atherton.

Bendick, Marc, Jr. 1983. "Government's Role in the Job Transitions of America's Dislocated Workers." Statement before the House Committee on Science and Technology and the House Committee on the Budget. Washington: Urban Institute, 9 June.

Bergsten, C. Fred. 1975a. "Economic Adjustment to Liberal Trade: A New Approach." In *Toward a New World Trade Policy: The Maidenhead Papers*. Edited by C. Fred Bergsten. Lexington, Mass.: Lexington Books, D. C. Heath and Co.

————. 1975b. "On the Non-Equivalence of Import Quotas and Voluntary Export Restraints." In *Toward a New World Trade Policy: The Maidenhead Papers*. Edited by C. Fred Bergsten. Lexington, Mass.: Lexington Books, D. C. Heath and Co.

————. 1985. "The Trade Deficit Could Be Ruinous." *Fortune*, 5 August.

Bergsten, C. Fred, and Gary C. Hufbauer. 1985. "A New Approach to Trade Adjustment Assistance." Statement before the Senate Finance Committee, Subcommittee on International Trade. Washington, 17 September.

Bhagwati, Jagdish N. 1982. "Shifting Comparative Advantage, Protectionist Demands, and Policy Response." In *Import Competition and Response*. Edited by Jagdish N. Bhagwati. National Bureau of Economic Research Conference Report. Chicago: University of Chicago Press.

Bluestone, Barry, Bennett Harrison, and Lucy Gorham. 1984. "Storm Clouds on the Horizon: Labor Market Crisis and Industrial Policy." Brookline, Mass.: Economic Education Project, May.

Bronckers, M. C. E. J. 1985. *Selective Safeguard Measures in Multilateral Trade Relations*. The Hague: T. M. C. Asser Instituut.

Cable, Vincent. 1983. *Protectionism and Industrial Decline*. London: Hodder and Stoughton for the Overseas Development Institute.

————. 1986. "Troubled Industries in the United Kingdom." In *Domestic Adjustment and International Trade*. Edited by Gary Clyde Hufbauer and Howard F. Rosen. Washington: Institute for International Economics, forthcoming.

Cable, Vincent, and Martin Weale. 1983. "Economic Costs of Sectoral Protection in Britain." *The World Economy*, vol. 6, no. 4 (December).

Cassing, James, Timothy J. McKeown, and Jack Ochs. 1984. "Firms, Regions, Business Cycles, and the Demand for Tariffs." Paper read at the Annual Meeting of the American Political Science Association. University of Pittsburgh, Pa., September.

Caves, Richard E., and Masu Uekusa. 1976. *Industrial Organization in Japan*. Washington: Brookings Institution.

Center for National Policy. 1984. *Promoting Economic Growth and Competitiveness*. Report of the Industry Policy Study Group. Washington, January.

Charnovitz, Steve. 1981. "The Tragedy of Trade Adjustment Assistance." US Department of Labor, Bureau of International Affairs. Washington, February.

————. 1984. "Trade Adjustment Assistance: What Went Wrong?" *Journal of the Institute for Socioeconomic Studies*, vol. 9, no. 1 (Spring).

Choate, Pat, Dennis Carey, and Malcolm Lovell. 1984. "Structural Change and Worker Displacement." Discussion paper for the Study Group on US Trade and Adjustment Policy, Council on Foreign Relations. Washington, 27 February.

Cline, William R. 1984a. "US Trade and Industrial Policy: The Experience of Textiles, Steel, and Automobiles." Paper read at Trade 1984, Conference Marking the 50th Anniversary of the US Export–Import Bank. Washington, October.

―――. 1984b. *Exports of Manufactures from Developing Countries: Performance and Prospects for Market Access.* Washington: Brookings Institution.

Collyns, Charles. 1982. *Can Protection Cure Unemployment?* Thames Essay No. 31. London: Trade Policy Research Centre.

Cooper, Ann. 1986. "Salvaging Trade Aid." *National Journal,* 11 January.

Cordes, Joseph J., Robert S. Goldfarb, and James R. Barth. 1983. "Compensating When the Government Harms." In *What Rules for Government?* Edited by R. Zeckhauser and Derek Leebaert. Durham, N.C.: Duke University Press.

Corson, Walter, Walter Nicholson, J. David Richardson, and Andre Vayda. 1979. *Final Report: Survey of Trade Adjustment Assistance Recipients.* Report to the Office of Foreign Economic Affairs, Bureau of International Labor Affairs, US Department of Labor. Princeton, N. J.: Mathematica Policy Research, Inc., December.

Cprek, Kent G. 1979. "Worker Adjustment Assistance: Black Comedy in the Post-Renaissance." *Law and Policy in International Business,* vol. 11.

Crandall, Robert. 1986. "Adjustment in the US Steel Industry." In *Domestic Adjustment and International Trade.* Edited by Gary Clyde Hufbauer and Howard F. Rosen. Washington: Institute for International Economics, forthcoming.

Data Resources, Inc. 1984. *The DRI Report on US Manufacturing.* New York: McGraw-Hill.

De Sola Pool, Ithiel, Hillard Rouncy, and Gilbert Scharfenberger. 1974. "The Working of Trade Adjustment Assistance at the Grass Roots Level." Report for the Department of Labor. Cambridge, Mass.: Massachusetts Institute of Technology, Center for International Business, December.

Destler, I. M. 1986. "Trade Adjustment Assistance in the American Political Environment." In *Domestic Adjustment and International Trade.* Edited by Gary Clyde Hufbauer and Howard F. Rosen. Washington: Institute for International Economics, forthcoming.

Dexter, Lewis Anthony. 1981. "Undesigned Consequences of Purposive Legislative Action: Alternatives to Implementation." *Journal of Public Policy,* vol. 1, no. 4 (October).

Dicke, Hugo, and Hans H. Glismann. 1986. "Troubled Industries in Germany." In *Domestic Adjustment and International Trade.* Edited by Gary Clyde Hufbauer and Howard F. Rosen. Washington: Institute for International Economics, forthcoming.

Eizenstat, Stuart E. 1984. "A Quid Pro Quo for Steel." *New York Times,* 18 September, A27.

Frank, Charles R. 1973. *Adjustment Assistance: American Jobs and Trade with the Developing Countries.* Development Paper no. 13. Overseas Development Council. Washington, June.

―――. 1977. *Foreign Trade and Domestic Aid.* Washington: Brookings Institution.

GATT Secretariat. 1978. "Modalities of Application of Article XIX." Report L/4679. Geneva, 5 July.

Goldfarb, Robert S. 1980. "Compensating Victims of Policy Change." *Regulation,* September/October.

Gordon, Michael R. 1980. "Trade Adjustment Assistance Program May be Too Big for Its Own Good." *National Journal,* 10 May.

Graham, Edward M. 1984. "Organized Labor and US International Economic Policy, 1881–1981." Chapel Hill, N. C.: University of North Carolina, forthcoming.

Gray, H. Peter, Thomas Pugel, and Ingo Walter. 1982. "International Trade, Employment and Structural Adjustment: The Case of the United States." International Labor Organization, World Employment Programme Research Working Paper no. WEP 2–36/WP 18. Geneva, July.

Gregory, R. G. 1976. "Some Implications of the Growth of the Mineral Sector." Australian Journal of Agricultural Economics, vol. 20 (August).

———. 1986. "Troubled Industries in Australia." In Domestic Adjustment and International Trade. Edited by Gary Clyde Hufbauer and Howard F. Rosen. Washington: Institute for International Economics, forthcoming.

Hamilton, Alexander. 1968. "Report on the Subject of Manufactures." In Industrial and Commercial Correspondence of Alexander Hamilton Anticipating His Report on Manufactures. Edited by Arthur Harrison Cole. New York: A. M. Kelley.

Heinz, John. 1983. "Industrial Revitalization Act of 1983." Congressional Record, vol. 129, no. 35 (18 March).

Horst, Thomas. 1986. "Income Tax Consequences for Corporations and Individuals Leaving Troubled Industries." In Domestic Adjustment and International Trade. Edited by Gary Clyde Hufbauer and Howard F. Rosen. Washington: Institute for International Economics, forthcoming.

Hufbauer, Gary Clyde, and Howard F. Rosen. 1983. "Managing Comparative Disadvantage." Washington: Institute for International Economics, June.

———, eds. 1986. Domestic Adjustment and International Trade. Washington: Institute for International Economics, forthcoming.

Hufbauer, Gary Clyde, and Andrew James Samet. 1985. "Trade Adjustment Assistance: Addressing the Consequences of International Competition." In International Trade Policy: A Lawyer's Perspective. Edited by John H. Jackson, Richard Cunningham, and Claude Fontheim. Washington: American Bar Association.

Hufbauer, Gary Clyde, and Jeffrey J. Schott. 1985. Trading for Growth: The Next Round of Trade Negotiations. POLICY ANALYSES IN INTERNATIONAL ECONOMICS 11. Washington: Institute for International Economics, September.

Hufbauer, Gary Clyde, Diane T. Berliner, and Kimberly Ann Elliott. 1986. Trade Protection in the United States: 31 Case Studies. Washington: Institute for International Economics.

Jackson, John H. 1986. "The Role of GATT in Monitoring Safeguards and Promoting Adjustment." In Domestic Adjustment and International Trade. Edited by Gary Clyde Hufbauer and Howard F. Rosen. Washington: Institute for International Economics, forthcoming.

Johnson, W., A. J. Sarna, and H. Kranklis. 1981. "The Impact of Multilateral Trade Negotiations on Industrial Adjustment." Trade and Structural Analysis Directorate, Office of Policy Analysis, Industry Trade and Commerce Department. Ottawa, Canada.

Kolberg, William H., ed. 1983. The Dislocated Worker. Cabin John, Md.: Seven Locks Press.

Krueger, Anne O. 1980. "Protectionist Pressures, Imports and Employment in the United States." Scandinavian Journal of Economics, pp. 133–46.

Kwoka, John E., Jr. 1986. "Antitrust Policy and Foreign Competition." In Domestic Adjustment and International Trade. Edited by Gary Clyde Hufbauer and Howard F. Rosen. Washington: Institute for International Economics, forthcoming.

Labor-Industry Coalition for International Trade. 1983. *International Trade, Industrial Policies, and the Future of American Industry.* Washington, April.

Lawrence, Robert Z. 1984. *Can America Compete?* Washington: Brookings Institution.

Lawrence, Robert Z., and Robert E. Litan. 1985. "Living with the Trade Deficit: Adjustment Strategies to Preserve Free Trade." *The Brookings Review,* vol. 4, no. 1 (Fall).

Lawrence, Robert Z., and Paula DeMasi. 1986. "The Adjustment Experience of Escape Clause Relief." In *Domestic Adjustment and International Trade.* Edited by Gary Clyde Hufbauer and Howard F. Rosen. Washington: Institute for International Economics, forthcoming.

McDowell, S., and P. Draper. 1978. *Trade Adjustment and the British Jute Industry.* London: Overseas Development Institute.

Magaziner, Ira, and Robert Reich. 1982. *Minding America's Business.* New York: Harcourt Brace Jovanovich.

Magee, Stephen P. 1980. "Three Simple Tests of the Stoper–Samuelson Theorem." In *Issues in International Economics.* Edited by P. Oppenheimer. London: Oriel Press.

Marris, Stephen. 1983. "Policies of Adjustment: The Role of the Economist." Paris: OECD, January.

————. 1985. *Deficits and the Dollar: The World Economy at Risk.* POLICY ANALYSES IN INTERNATIONAL ECONOMICS 14. Washington: Institute for International Economics, December.

Martin, Phillip L. 1983. *Labor Displacement and Public Policy.* Lexington, Mass.: D. C. Heath and Co.

Messerlin, Patrick A. 1981. "The Political Economy of Protectionism: The Bureaucratic Case." *Weltwirtschaftliches Archiv,* vol. 117, no. 3.

Metzger, Stanley D. 1964. *Trade Agreements and the Kennedy Round.* Fairfax, Va.: Coiner Publications.

————. 1971a. "Adjustment Assistance." In *United States International Economic Policy in an Interdependent World: Compendium of Papers.* Vol. 1. Washington: President's Commission on International Trade and Investment Policy (Williams Commission), July.

————. 1971b. "Injury and Market Disruption from Imports." In *United States International Economic Policy in an Interdependent World: Compendium of Papers.* Vol. 1. Washington: President's Commission on International Trade and Investment Policy (Williams Commission), July.

Miles, Caroline. 1968. *Lancashire Textiles: A Case Study of Industrial Change.* Cambridge: Cambridge University Press.

Mitchell, Daniel J. B. 1976. "Is Adjustment Assistance an Answer?" *California Management Review,* vol. 19, no. 2 (Winter).

Munger, Michael C. 1983. *The Costs of Protectionism: Estimates of the Hidden Tax of Trade Restraint.* Working Paper no. 80. Washington University, Center for the Study of American Business, July.

Mutti, John, and Howard F. Rosen. 1986. "US Labor Market Adjustment." In *Domestic Adjustment and International Trade.* Edited by Gary Clyde Hufbauer and Howard F. Rosen. Washington: Institute for International Economics, forthcoming.

Orr, Ann C., and James A. Orr. 1983. "Employment Adjustments in Import-Sensitive Manufacturing Industries, 1960–1980." Prepared for the Annual Meeting of the Industrial Relations Research Association. San Francisco, December.

Orr, James A. 1984. "A Strategic Approach to the Problems of Depressed Industries: Lessons from Foreign Experiences." Discussion paper for the Study Group on US Trade and Adjustment Policy, Council on Foreign Relations. Washington, 9 April.

―――. 1986. "US Policies for Displaced Workers." In *Domestic Adjustment and International Trade*. Edited by Gary Clyde Hufbauer and Howard F. Rosen. Washington: Institute for International Economics, forthcoming.

Personick, Valerie A. 1983. "The Job Outlook through 1995: Industry Output and Employment." *Monthly Labor Review*, vol. 106, no. 11 (November).

Podgursky, Michael. 1984. "Labor Market Policy and Structural Adjustment." In *Policies for Industrial Growth in a Competitive World*. Prepared for US Congress, Joint Economic Committee. 98 Cong., 2d. sess., April.

Preeg, Ernest H. 1970. *Traders and Diplomats*. Washington: Brookings Institution.

Price, Lee. 1984. "Trade Issues in Industrial Policy." In *Policies for Industrial Growth in a Competitive World*. Prepared for US Congress, Joint Economic Committee. 98 Cong., 2d sess., April.

Pugel, Thomas A., and Ingo Walter. 1983. "US Corporate Interests and the Political Economy of Trade Policy." New York University, Graduate School of Business Administration, December.

Richardson, J. David. 1982. "Trade Adjustment Assistance Under the Trade Act of 1974." In *Import Competition and Response*. Edited by Jagdish N. Bhagwati. National Bureau of Economic Research Conference Report. Chicago: University of Chicago Press.

―――. 1982. "Worker Adjustment to US International Trade: Programs and Prospects." Prepared for the Conference on Trade Policy in the Eighties, Institute for International Economics. Washington, June.

Rosen, Howard F. 1985. "The Impact of International Trade on US Employment." Statement before the House Committee on Government Operations, Subcommittee on Employment and Housing. Washington, 3 October.

Rosenblatt, Samuel M. 1977. "Trade Adjustment Assistance Programs: Crossroads or Dead End?" *Law and Policy in International Business*, vol. 9, no. 3.

Schultz, Siegfried, and Dieter Schumacher. 1984. "The Re-liberalization of World Trade." *Journal of World Trade Law*, vol. 18, no. 3 (May/June).

Smith, Adam. 1880. *An Inquiry into the Nature and Causes of the Wealth of Nations*. 2d ed. Oxford: Clarendon Press.

Tribe, Lawrence. 1978. *American Constitutional Law*. Mineola, NY: Foundation Press.

US Congress. Joint Economic Committee. 1984. *Policies for Industrial Growth in a Competitive World*. Senate Report 98–187. 98 Cong., 2d sess., 27 April.

US Congressional Budget Office. 1982. *Dislocated Workers: Issues and Federal Options*. Washington, July.

―――. 1983. *The Industrial Policy Debate*. Washington, December.

―――. 1984. *Federal Support of US Business*. Washington, January.

US Congressional Research Service. 1984. "Agriculture in the GATT: Toward the Next Round of Multilateral Trade Negotiations." Report 84–169. Washington, September.

US Department of Interior. Bureau of Mines. 1983. *Chromium, Mineral Commodity Profile*. Washington.

US Department of Labor. Office of Foreign Economic Research, Bureau of International Labor Affairs. 1978. "The Impact of Changes in Manufacturing Trade on Sectoral Employment

Patterns—Progress Report.'' Prepared for the Conference on the Employment Effects of International Trade. Washington, November.

———. Bureau of Labor Statistics. 1985. *Displaced Workers, 1979–1983*. Bulletin 2240. Washington, July.

US General Accounting Office. 1978. *Adjustment Assistance to Firms Under the Trade Act of 1974—Income Maintenance or Successful Adjustment*. Report 10–78–53. Washington, December.

———. 1980. *Restricting Trade Act Benefits to Import-Affected Workers Who Cannot Find a Job Can Save Millions*. Washington, January.

———. 1981. *Changes Needed in Administering Relief to Industries Hurt by Overseas Competition*. Report ID–81–42. Washington, August.

US House of Representatives. 1982. *Trade Adjustment Assistance for Workers*. Hearing before the Subcommittee on Trade, Committee on Ways and Means. Serial 97–61. 97 Cong., 2d sess., 14 July.

———. 1983. *Worker and Firm Trade Adjustment Assistance*. House Report 98–281. 98 Cong., 1st sess., 29 June.

US International Trade Commission. 1981. *High Carbon Ferrochromium*. USITC Publication no. 1185. Washington, September.

———. 1982. *The Effectiveness of Escape Clause Relief in Promoting Adjustment Import Competition*. USITC Publication no. 1229. Washington, March.

———. 1983. *US Trade-Related Employment*. USITC Publication no. 1445. Washington.

———. 1984a. *Color Television Receivers from the Republic of Korea and Taiwan*. USITC Publication no. 1514. Washington, April.

———. 1984b. *Carbon and Certain Alloy Steel Products*. 2 vols. USITC Publication no. 1553. Washington, July.

———. 1984c. *Nonrubber Footwear*. USITC Publication no. 1545. Washington, July

———. 1985. *Nonrubber Footwear*. USITC Publication no. 1717. Washington, July.

US Trade Representative. 1984. *Annual Report of the President of the United States on the Trade Agreements Program, 1983*. Washington, April.

Vargo, Franklin J. 1971. ''How Others Do It. Trade Adjustment Assistance for Firms and Industries In: Belgium, Canada, France, Germany, Italy, Japan, Netherlands, Sweden, United Kingdom, European Community.'' Report ER-C9. Office of Economic Research, US Department of Commerce. Washington, May.

Walker, Gary, with William Grinker, Thomas Seessel, R. C. Smith, and Vincent Cama. 1984. *An Independent Sector Assessment of the Job Training Partnership Act, Phase I: The Initial Transition*. MDC, Inc., March.

Weil, Frank A. 1983. ''US Industrial Policy: A Process in Need of a Federal Industrial Coordination Board.'' *Law and Policy in International Business*, vol. 14, no. 4.

Williamson, John. 1985. *The Exchange Rate System*. 2d ed., rev. POLICY ANALYSES IN INTERNATIONAL ECONOMICS 5. Washington: Institute for International Economics, June.

International Debt: Systemic Risk and Policy Response
William R. Cline/1984

Economic Sanctions Reconsidered: History and Current Policy
Gary Clyde Hufbauer and Jeffrey J. Schott, assisted by Kimberly Ann Elliott/
1985

Trade Protection in the United States: 31 Case Studies
Gary Clyde Hufbauer, Diane T. Berliner, and Kimberly Ann Elliott/1986

SPECIAL REPORTS

1 **Promoting World Recovery: A Statement on Global Economic Strategy** *by Twenty-six Economists from Fourteen Countries*/December 1982

2 **Prospects for Adjustment in Argentina, Brazil, and Mexico: Responding to the Debt Crisis**
John Williamson, editor/June 1983

3 **Inflation and Indexation: Argentina, Brazil, and Israel**
John Williamson, editor/March 1985

4 **Global Economic Imbalances**
C. Fred Bergsten, editor/March 1986

FORTHCOMING

Domestic Adjustment and International Trade
Gary Clyde Hufbauer and Howard F. Rosen, editors

Toward A New Development Strategy for Latin America
Bela Balassa, Gerardo M. Bueno, Pedro-Pablo Kuczynski, and Mario Henrique Simonsen

Another Multi-Fiber Arrangement?
William R. Cline

The Politics of Anti-Protection
I. M. Destler and John S. Odell

Japan in the World Economy
Bela Balassa and Marcus Noland

International Trade in Automobiles: Liberalization or Further Restraint?
William R. Cline

The Multiple Reserve Currency System
C. Fred Bergsten and John Williamson

New International Arrangements for Foreign Direct Investment
C. Fred Bergsten and Jeffrey J. Schott

Toward Cartelization of World Steel Trade?
William R. Cline

Trade Controls in Three Industries: The Automobile, Steel, and Textiles Cases
William R. Cline